WHAT'S UP WITH THE
HARD CORE JEWISH PEOPLE?

(The Jewish Kid is the one on the cover with his hat on backwards and his tzitzis hanging out over his shorts.)

This is the first book about Observant Jews that is written from the perspective of a non-Observant person with a sassy attitude. It will capture the interest and entertain both Jews and non-Jews who want an easy way to learn more about Judaism.

Four years ago our youngest son, a graduate of the University of Pennsylvania, blew off law school and decided to study in Israel to be an Orthodox rabbi. What a ride it has been for our family trying to stay close to Carter, because we're Reform Jews and very different than him. Whenever I relate stories regarding incidents in our household or tidbits of Jewish knowledge I have acquired since Carter went Hard Core, regardless of age, gender, religion, or level of religious observance, people are always fascinated. It seems like everyone knows someone who has become more intensely religious in life, and they enjoy hearing how our family has coped with the situation.

10-Digit ISBN 1-59113-906-6
13-Digit ISBN 978-1-59113-906-5

Printed in the United States of America.

Booklocker.com, Inc.
2006

Library of Congress Cataloging-in-Publication Data

Schwartz, Margery Isis, 1949-
  What's up with the hard core Jewish people? : an irreverent yet informative approach to Judaism and religious devotion from a Reform Jewish mother's perspective / Margery Isis Schwartz.
      p. cm.
  Includes bibliographical references.
  ISBN-13: 978-1-59113-906-5 (alk. paper)
  ISBN-10: 1-59113-906-6
1. Jews--Return to Orthodox Judaism. 2. Orthodox Judaism--Relations--Nontraditional Jews. 3. Orthodox Judaism--Customs and practices. I. Title.

  BM565.S375 2006
  296.7'15--dc22

                                        2006006576

WHAT'S UP WITH THE
HARD CORE JEWISH PEOPLE?

An irreverent yet informative approach to Judaism
and religious devotion from a
Reform Jewish mother's perspective

Margery Isis Schwartz

TABLE OF CONTENTS

INTRODUCTION

According to one estimate, there are tens of thousands of Jews across North America who were raised by non-Orthodox parents, but decide to live as fully Observant Jews. They are returning to the ways not of their parents but of their grandparents and great-grandparents. These returnees are called *ba'al teshuva* (pronounced ball-CHOO-va) or BTs for short. The transformation from Secular to Observant Jew is rather shocking to those of us on the "dark side." When our son, Carter, decided to blow off law school and stay in Jerusalem and study to be an Orthodox Rabbi, we were in cognitive dissonance. In our wildest dreams, we would have never expected such a thing. Why would a comfortably affluent, well-educated, Secular Jew seek out the rigorous discipline of traditional Jewish observance?

I had no one to turn to for information but the Hard Core Jewish People, and they're no help. They thought what Carter was doing was the "bomb." They lauded him for his courage — the consequences be damned. What about living 7,000 miles away from home on a different continent? What about the U.S. Department of State Travel Warning urging U.S. citizens to carefully weigh the necessity of their travel to Israel in light of the suicide bombings that were taking place on a regular basis? What about the divisiveness such a drastic lifestyle change can cause in a family? None of that matters because *Torah* rules! By learning Torah, Carter would be another link in the unbroken chain carrying Jewish tradition along to the next generation. Oy!

What was it that gave our "lunatic" son the spirit of inquiry, the intense desire for truth, and the courage to begin a journey in which his long-neglected soul has grown from an atrophied state into an all-encompassing spirituality — to the point where the single most prominent characteristic of his identity is that of a religious Jew? I needed to understand what the hell just happened to our kid, why it happened, and what had to be done to keep Carter's desire to be an Observant Jew from breaking up our family. Losing our son to Judaism was not going to be an option.

It would have been great if there was a cram course or CliffNotes on the rules and regulations involved in *halacha* (ha-LOCK-ha; Jewish law). But there was no such course and no simple to-the-point book that would expediently teach me about Judaism and what I needed to do in order for Carter to feel comfortable at our house. All of the books available about BTs and Judaism are by rabbis, BTs, or other Observant Jews whose perspective is very different than mine. Furthermore, they tell us way more than we want or need to know, and typically include terminology that is foreign and nearly incomprehensible to non-Observant Jews like me. I did extensive reading and research on the Internet and felt compelled to write this book: (1) To share my story and provide the reader with consolation, guidance, entertainment, and suggestions on how to deal with a formerly non-religious Jew who has become Orthodox, and

(2) To impart my Jewish knowledge in a user-friendly way and help people understand what it means to be Jewish. While the jocular, irreverent approach I've used in the book reflects my personality, it is also intended to help maintain the reader's interest and put a smile on your face. I have a great deal of respect for the Jewish People and in no way do I intend for these words to denigrate them or their ancient religion and customs.

Note: When I refer to <u>the Jewish People</u>, it is a reference to the Jews as a nation in the classical sense, meaning a group of people with a shared history and a sense of a group identity rather than a territorial and political entity. The Jewish People have pride in their heritage and an affinity for Israel. By the term <u>Hard Core Jewish People</u>, I mean those who intensely commit themselves to following Jewish law. Words written in italics are defined in Section III, the Glossary.

The book is divided into three sections. Section I deals with my personal journey as our youngest son became a Hard Core Jewish Kid. Section II presents everything you ever wanted to know about Judaism without really trying, and Section III is a very handy Jewish dictionary.

SECTION I: THE STORY

How The Hell Did This Happen In Our Family?

Knowing our family and the manner in which our children were raised, no one could have possibly anticipated that one of our offspring would become an Observant Jew. From our children's names alone, it is evident that Barry and I are children of the 60's. We've got our oldest son, Tyler Blue, a flower-child who lives in Santa Barbara with his non-Jewish fiancé, Raven. They adhere to the philosophy of "live for today" and "go for the moment." Tyler and Raven met at a Phish concert several years ago. After Tyler graduated from Clemson University, they began living together in Santa Barbara in 1999 and have a very loving relationship. They adore their two dogs, share a passion for live music, and enjoy the activities and friends that life in California affords them. Tyler is a freelance writer for a variety of publications. Raven is a non-denominational wedding minister who performs beautiful custom-designed ceremonies for that special day. She is also an herbalist who specializes in the medicinal use of plants and treating the whole person rather than just the symptom. The extent of Tyler and Raven's acknowledgment of a Higher Being is celebrating Chanukah, having a Seder on the first night of Passover, and their custom of waving their hands over their plates before they eat a meal.

On the other side of the world is Carter Sky, two and a half years younger than Tyler, who lives in Jerusalem and is studying to be an Orthodox rabbi. No one would have ever

3

expected Carter to take on a *Torah*-centric lifestyle, chock full of stringent guidelines that dictate how he should lead his life. Carter was never a submissive and obedient individual. It was always a challenge being his parent. He was strong-willed from birth, and our household revolved around him in order to keep the peace. As Carter went, so went the Schwartz family. He was in the terrible two's for about five years. I remember trying to get him dressed so we could meet friends or go to an appointment, and he would insist upon putting on his own shoes. "Cartie do," he would say as he obstinately tried to get the shoes on his feet, even though a two year old can't easily do such a task. I would say to him: "Carter, you're being argumentative, cantankerous, and belligerent." He was so precocious that after I said those three words enough times and in the same type of situation, I could ask Carter what he was being and in his little voice he would say, "Argumentative, cantankerous, and belligerent." Sometimes he was such a terror that I told him he'd need to have a lucrative profession when he grew up in order to buy gifts for his wife to apologize to her for insults or other negative behaviors. Subsequently when people asked Carter what he was going to do when he grew up, he'd say in his little boy voice, "I'm going to have a lucrative profession."

As a young adult, Carter was this charismatic guy who one would find in the VIP rooms at South Beach's finest clubs when he was home on college breaks. He was a fraternity guy at the University of Pennsylvania who could party hardy; he knew how to have a good time. He was Mr. Body Beautiful who worked out faithfully and sculpted his body to a masterpiece. For Carter's 21st birthday, we rented a bus and Carter, Tyler, and a busload of friends went to South Beach clubbing. No one had to worry about driving under the influence and we had three ice chests filled with water, alcohol, soft drinks, and food to keep them going all night. It was a party to remember. It's amazing how so much can change in two years. It's still difficult for us to fathom that this free-spending guy is now someone who prefers living a minimal material life and focusing on more spiritual and moral values. Who'd of thunk such a thing could happen?

Barry, my husband of 35 years, is a soft-spoken level-headed guy with a Ph.D. in Experimental Psychology. After working at Burger King Corporation for 19 years as their Director of Consumer Research, Barry came on board at ASPEN RESEARCH, a marketing research company I founded in January 1991. He works out of the home office while my office is in Coral Gables. Because of our reputation, experience, and mission of quality and excellence, word-of-mouth keeps the business flowing in without the necessity of cold calls. We are empty-nesters living the Life of Riley in my opinion. It's just like when we were first married except we have a lot more money now. To have no child-rearing responsibilities feels like such a victory — we did it! Now we're free.

I'm a wild woman with a zest for life and am appreciative for everything. "Girls Just Wanna Have Fun" is my theme song and it's not unusual to find me shimmying through the house to the sound of Mitch Ryder & the Detroit Wheels "Devil

With a Blue Dress On." Barry calls me his high school daughter because I still shriek when I hear a great song come on and view life through the eyes of a teenager. I drive around in my 2006 330i Bimmer listening to my iPod playing "We Are Family" or some other oldie, and I'll look up through my sunroof and say, "Thank you, *Hashem* (another word for God)." Okay, so I pay homage to Hashem in a different and more spontaneous way than the Hard Cores.

Being products of our environment, Barry and I are casual Jews, viewing ourselves as Americans first and Jews second. Like our assimilated parents, culture has replaced tradition and spirituality has replaced religion. While we regard being Jewish as central to our being, we are unwilling to devote ourselves to Torah law, customs of praying, and praising Hashem on an ongoing basis. It wasn't until Carter became a Hard Core Jewish Kid that I realized I was functionally illiterate with regard to *Jewish values*, tradition, and history.

Our children attended a Reform Jewish day school from nursery school through sixth grade, and we were members of a Reform synagogue. We frequented services on Yom Kippur and Rosh Hashanah and would go to our friends' house each year for the first night of Passover. Tyler had his Bar Mitzvah at Temple Beth Am in Miami and had a celebration afterwards at the Hyatt Hotel in Coral Gables. My dad and my father-in-law were still alive and well and able to attend and participate in the ceremony and festivities. Barry's mother died when he was a senior in high school and my mom passed away when Carter was two months old. Carter's Bar Mitzvah was in Aspen, Colorado because by then, both of my parents were dead and my father-in-law had Alzheimer's. I knew that their presence would be greatly missed, and I didn't want us to be sad. Since Aspen is one of our favorite places on earth, that seemed like a good place for us to be. My brother and his family, my sister and her daughter, a few friends, and some other relatives joined us in Aspen for a very warm and loving ceremony and celebration. After their Bar Mitzvah, we didn't force the boys to attend Confirmation classes at the synagogue. For me, Confirmation classes were a social thing and I didn't learn much, so I spared both of our boys from that obligation.

We had a Christmas tree every year because my dad wouldn't let me have one when I was growing up, and I love to see the twinkling lights. Since a Christmas tree is not treated as an idol but rather a temporary fragrant fixture, I figured it couldn't do any harm. One time Carter slipped and told his Jewish day school teacher or his teacher overheard that we had a tree. I got a phone call from the school's religious director inquiring, "Mrs. Schwartz: Don't you think you're confusing your children by having a Christmas tree?" I said, "No, the boys know that when pineapples are in season we have pineapples. And when Christmas trees are in season, we have a tree. It's not a religious thing for us." I asked the boys, "Does the fact that we have a Christmas tree confuse you about your being Jewish?" And those little angels said, "No Mommy, we're not confused." So annually I got to have my twinkling lights until Carter became a Hard Core

Jewish Kid. Out of respect for his beliefs and those of the Jewish People, I gave away all the beautiful ornaments we had accumulated over 32 years. Oh well, things could be worse.

Our family was always very close and now I thank my lucky stars for all the years we were together. I didn't know that our boys would leave us and be so far away when they became adults. No one warned me about that. I was like Earth Mother when they were born. Neither child ever had a bottle of milk or a jar of baby food. I even made their teething biscuits with soy flour and molasses. We took the boys with us on all our vacations because we loved being with them. In addition to multitudes of trips to Disney World, they joined us in places like Las Vegas, Maui, Europe, and we went skiing together in Aspen, Vail, Steamboat, Beaver Creek, Lake Tahoe, and even Zermatt, Switzerland. When Carter was in London for his semester abroad, Tyler flew in from Santa Barbara and we flew in from Miami and we all converged there for Thanksgiving. Up until January 2002 when Carter left for Israel, we were a seemingly normal family to the untrained eye. We had no idea that our youngest son was on the verge of a drastic lifestyle change that would challenge the solidarity of our family.

Carter's Path to Becoming a Hard Core Jewish Kid

The Scenario

People are always asking me what prompted Carter to become an Observant Jew. Based on Carter's metamorphosis as well as that of many others I've observed, it's never just one moment of truth or a single "aha" revelation that drives someone to become a committed Jew. It seems to be a process – an evolution of the soul or successive approximations that reinforce them for getting closer to God. Everyone's story is different and unique, but the one commonality is a search for meaning and truth. As for Carter, he was always thinking about things beyond his years and interested in understanding the various religions and spirituality. When he was growing up, the Jehovah's Witnesses used to come to our house and ask for Carter specifically. While at the University of Pennsylvania (UPenn), which has a large percentage of Jewish students, Carter was exposed to many people who were more observant than him. He realized that he had never experienced the spiritual side of Judaism. He wanted to learn more about his faith and Jewish heritage.

In the summer after his sophomore year, Carter went on the March of the Living – a well known organized trip geared to exposing high school and college students to the atrocities of the Holocaust. The journey included visiting the concentration camps of Auschwitz, Birkenau, Treblinka, and Majdanek in Poland. Holocaust survivors gave personal accounts of what they saw, witnessed, and experienced, and this magnified the horror of the reality. Their last stop was Israel, where they visited key sights. The purpose of the mission was to "create memories, leading to a revitalized commitment to Judaism, Israel, and the Jewish People." Carter is one of their success stories because he returned from that trip with a strengthened Jewish identity, increased Jewish pride, and an affinity for Israel as the Jewish State. But he was still a Secular Jew and could be as much of a "wild man" as he ever was.

During his junior year at UPenn, Carter attended some events at the Chabad House. Chabad is an educational outreach organization dedicated to spreading Jewish knowledge, enthusiasm, and pride. Their goal is to serve the spiritual needs of each Jew, regardless of background or affiliation. From the first moment Carter stepped into the door at Chabad, he felt completely accepted even though he wasn't an Observant Jew. The wine and vodka they served there increased the appeal, and provided yet another good reason to visit. One of the rabbis at the Chabad encouraged Carter to pursue Jewish spirituality — to become aware of God's presence and purpose. It was at this point that Carter started learning about the symbolic meaning behind *Torah* laws, finding the ideas and philosophy deep and meaningful.

For the first semester of his senior year, Carter attended King's College in London, England to study at their

Department of War Studies. Carter has always been interested in the many facets of war in terms of historical and contemporary settings, strategies, and moral judgment. One of his close friends from UPenn joined him in London, and they spent a lot of time together. Jon was raised in an Orthodox home, but was rebelling somewhat now that he was on his own. Jon had several Orthodox relatives living in London and he and Carter spent many *Shabbat* dinners with these people. Carter saw the closeness and warmth of Jewish families and the Jewish community, and he found their intellect, ethics, and values compelling.

Returning from London for his final semester at UPenn, Carter wasn't at all sure what he wanted to do upon graduation. He knew that he didn't want to automatically matriculate to law school or graduate school or a job on Wall Street like many of his friends. He was looking for his purpose in life; he was in search of meaning. In May 2001, Carter graduated from the University of Pennsylvania with a 3.6 GPA. After graduation, he first considered film school and was studying to take the GRE required for admissions.

On September 11, 2001, Carter watched the horror of the events unfold on television and couldn't pull himself away. It was too mind-boggling to think that thousands of people went to work that day or got on a plane and would never be returning home again to their loved ones. What legacy did these people leave behind? Is that all there is to life – one minute we're alive and the next minute we're dead? Two days later, Carter was studying for LSAT exams, which are required for admission to law school. He wanted to be in a decision-making position to influence government policies and strategies to prevent terrorist acts from occurring again on U.S. soil.

While Carter was home in Miami, he was going through a Jewish transition. He felt a hunger and a strong desire to connect more with Judaism. Slowly but surely, he started performing *mitzvot* (Torah obligations) such as eating *kosher* (when it was convenient – he was flexible if necessary). Every weekend he would observe the *Sabbath* and then go nightclubbing on South Beach on Saturday night. On weekdays he spent time learning about Judaism with a charismatic rabbi at Young Israel of Kendall. The rabbi recommended that before Carter started law school, he should spend some time in Israel at a *yeshiva* (Jewish learning institution) that caters to connecting disenfranchised Jews to their heritage. There he could study Torah and infuse himself with Jewish spirituality before heading off to law school.

Carter sent applications to 14 law schools and then left in January 2002 for a three to five month trip to Israel to explore his Jewish roots. We didn't know that he had another agenda. "Mom, when will I have another opportunity to do something like this?" "But Carter," I said, "it's such a dangerous time now in Jerusalem. Suicide bombings are a regular occurrence and there are a lot of us who won't be doing very well if anything happens to you." No matter what we said or tried to bribe him with to keep him from going to The Promised Land, Carter would not be deterred. We could never have predicted that the next time we would see our son he would be a Hard Core Jewish Kid — a person whose life revolves around following all of the rules and regulations of the Torah.

People thought we were crazy "to let our son" go to such a dangerous place, but timeouts aren't effective on 22-year-olds. Unfortunately, when he left for Israel, it was during the second Palestinian intifada (pronounced in-ti-FA-da; a reign of terror). The Palestinians were trying to demoralize Israel and destroy its economy by killing innocent people using suicide bombers. The violence spiraled to an all-time high in March 2002 when 124 people were killed and 609 injured. This included a suicide bomber killing 11 at a crowded café on Ben Yehuda St. in Jerusalem, 29 Jews killed at a Passover Seder at a hotel in Netanya, and 20 mostly women and small children killed at a Jerusalem bus stop. We were trying to be calm about the whole thing. Carter was on a mission to learn about Judaism and our job was to handle it. Barry and I attended the Coconut Grove Art Show and were walking around, holding hands like we were normal people. I turned and said to him, "How many parents whose kids are sitting in a yeshiva in Jerusalem are walking around peacefully instead of being bedridden with fear that their child's life is in danger from Palestinian extremists?" Fortunately, Carter had taught us right off the bat that everything that happens is in *Hashem's* hands so if it's meant to be, it's meant to be. Got it! We'll be cool. Not to worry. I told Carter: "Just stay in the Old City at your yeshiva and keep studying. If you need anything, just tell me and I'll send it. Whatever you do, don't take a bus anywhere and don't go to Ben Yehuda Street." I was consoled knowing that Carter's passion for learning Torah kept him in a protected area most of the time. The Old City of East Jerusalem where he lived at Aish HaTorah contains historic buildings and monuments that are sacred to Muslims and Jews alike, and the security is very heavy. At least he wasn't bee-bopping around town.

There we were, living in a different hemisphere, getting acceptance letters right and left from the various law schools to which Carter applied, and our kid is studying Torah at Aish HaTorah in Jerusalem and falling deeper in love with Judaism. Carter's grades, LSAT scores, and other credentials were so impressive that UCLA, USC, and George Washington University offered him unsolicited scholarships. In our frequent communications with him, I took on the role of devil's advocate to try and keep him focused on not putting law school on the back burner. After all, Carter was surrounded by people who were telling him that he was exactly where he belonged and doing exactly what he should be doing. In the Torah view, the most important people alive are Torah scholars. Torah study is essential to the life of a serious Jew because that is the only way they know how God wants them to live their lives. But it doesn't pay the bills. Somebody had to speak out against the madness. The families of BTs (newly Observant Jews) are typically ignorant of basic Judaism and we have no leg to stand on when being admonished for just how non-spiritual our lives are and how great it is to be an Observant Jew. I did a great deal of Internet research to learn about Judaism and Torah law, because one needs to speak to Hard Cores on their terms in order to be at all convincing. I would say things to Carter like, "It's a good thing that you're going into law because the hundreds of Jewish women who have been denied a divorce document (i.e., a "Get") by their husbands need someone to speak up for them. Then I'd verbally attack the *Haredim* (pronounced ha-REE-dim; Torah-true/God-fearing Jews) who got the Egged Bus Service in Jerusalem to require women to sit at the back of the bus on two Hard Core Jewish routes. I said, "Rosa Parks' hair would go straight if she heard about this. What's the deal with these guys? They can't control themselves around women so they want women out of their view? Why can't they handle it like the rest of the guys in the world?"

I thought it seemed ironic that the Torah, which preaches that we should love others as we love ourselves and puts honoring one's parents in the Ten Commandments — and on the first of the two tablets no less — should produce so much strife among family members by encouraging lifestyle overhauls for individuals. I learned quickly, however, not to bother using the commandment "Honor thy mother and father" for ammunition to get our kid to come home. Studying Torah leaves that *mitzvah* (Torah obligation) in the dirt. The Torah says, "Honor your father and mother, I am Hashem." What that actually translates to is: obey your parents in all things, except when they command you to transgress the Torah. Once the BT becomes aware of Jewish law and sees the beauty, value, and truth of the teachings of

Torah, he/she wants to repent and live a Torah-true life. This is called *teshuva* — being sorry for having disobeyed God and remedying that fault by being a servant of God. You'd have to kill them to get them to stop following Torah. The harsh reality is that they are even willing to discard their birth family if that's what it takes to live the way they know God wants them to. Emotions, logic, and sentimentality have no place in Torah-true Judaism.

Aish HaTorah, Carter's yeshiva that specializes in BTs, uses an intellectual approach that is particularly appealing to the many secular well-educated Americans it seeks to attract. To prove the divine origin of the Torah, Aish teaches their students about "hidden codes" in the Book of Genesis" which foresaw information about people, places and events that happened much, much later than when it was written. This scientifically substantiates the fact that God is real and the Torah is from God and thus it is the truth and the ultimate objective guide for how human beings should conduct their lives. God sustains the universe every second – every creature, every blade of grass. God makes your heart pump. He provides your food. He created the sun to provide heat and light. There is nothing that can stop God. Every single thing we have is sent from God. Accordingly, Hard Core Jewish People are committed to paying homage to God 24/7 to show their gratitude and appreciation for the goodness and loving-kindness that they believe He showers upon them.

When Carter was convinced of the authenticity of God, this meant that he also had to take the Covenant seriously. The

Covenant is the commitment the Jews made to God to become the teachers of His morality – Torah. In return, the Jews would be blessed with God's love and protection if they remained true to God's law, and faithfully worshipped Him. They would also be held accountable for sins and transgressions against God and His laws. The Torah was offered to all nations of the world but because of *Abraham's* dedication and willingness to give up everything for God, he was chosen along with his descendents. Thus Jews are considered the *"Chosen People"* because of their willingness to accept those duties, which the rest of the world rejected. We really can't blame our ancestors for unconditionally, wholeheartedly, sight-unseen, committing themselves to following the manifold dictates of the Torah. It had to be an awesome scene when God revealed Himself to all who had gathered at Mt. Sinai. They saw and heard God speak. From the Orthodox perspective, all Jews are included in the Covenant, regardless of whether we consciously affirm it, whether we identify as ethnic Secular Jews, or whether we are indifferent to our Jewishness. [Be grateful for the Hard Core Jewish People who are willing to abide by the Covenant, because at least somebody is doing it. Most of us refuse to take responsibility for something we didn't personally commit to. Instead we'll live life on the edge and deal with any repercussions later.]

As May approached, the time we expected Carter to return home, he informed us that he had decided not to go to law school and instead stay at Aish and study to become an Orthodox rabbi. We gave it our best shot once again in trying to dissuade him with every form of bribery possible, but Carter stood firm in his decision to become a committed Torah Jew. The yeshiva is very adept at preparing BTs to defend their new passion for learning Torah. They encourage students to reject their upbringing if it's not according to Torah. They believe that they are reprogramming our children on the proper path. Aish doesn't focus on the fact that a person from a non-Orthodox background most often cannot be integrated into the ultra-Orthodox world without destroying old friendships and even family connections. Relationships with families can become strained as relatives may not eat on the same family dinnerware (due to dietary rules) or be together with families on the Sabbath and holidays. Old friends may be cut off as the BT increasingly only associates with others who observe Orthodox Judaism at a similar level. Some BTs decide to use their Hebrew names, even more symbolically cutting ties with their old lifestyle. The toll such transformations exact can be staggering. Oh well. La-dee-da! They're following Torah so handle it.

We knew Carter was a goner when he told us he was *shomer negiah* (show-MARE ne-GEE-uh). This means that other than a mother, grandmother, or sister (of which he has none), Carter can't touch or be touched by a woman to whom he is not married. Even shaking hands is out of the question, which can be very offensive to people not familiar with that Torah law. When dating, couples are not allowed to hold hands, hug, kiss, or see each other naked until they are married. The problem is that we are a very huggy-kissy family, and Carter had always been a huggy-kissy guy. When we see friends, we hug. When we see relatives, we hug. Now Carter can no longer hug his aunts, his female cousins, or his female friends because of shomer negiah. I view shomer negiah as being one of those Jewish laws that has the potential to hurt people's feelings by making them feel rejected. One explanation given for why God would include this law in the Torah is to discourage a hug or a handshake from leading to thinking lustful thoughts. Since it's in the Torah and Hard Core Jewish People do not want to deviate from the Torah because they might dilute Judaism and then be like us, it doesn't matter what I think. Torah rules and logic and emotions should be suppressed. I get it but I don't agree with it. Even Carter was amazed when he became shomer negiah. He had become aware of this law, but initially couldn't imagine himself observing it. Being kosher and celebrating Shabbat was one thing, but shomer negiah...? He ultimately succumbed.

When we finally acknowledged the amount of courage, discipline, and determination it had required on Carter's part to resist peer and parental pressure and adhere to living a Jewish life, it became clear to us that he was truly committed to following Torah. Our job was to go into what I refer to as "Xanax-mode" (staying calm as if on this popular anti-depressant no mtter how preposterous something sounds) and my new favorite word became "whatever." We have always shown enthusiasm in our children's interests that were advantageous to their futures, and we also live by the philosophy of accepting each other unconditionally. Going into my defense mechanism mode, I convinced myself that Carter may be different than us, but not bad different. I was determined to figure out a way to keep the peace. If our son was blind, I'd learn Braille. Now that Carter was an Orthodox Jew, we had to start learning about Judaism so we could be on the same wavelength. I also needed to know the rules and regulations involved in *halacha* (Jewish law) in order to create an environment in our house such that Carter would be free to come home for a visit without us having to become kosher and Observant Jews. I'm too hedonistic to consider a pious existence.

Is Orthodox Jewish Outreach a Cult?

Aish HaTorah (Aish), the Jewish educational institute (yeshiva) where Carter ended up when he got to Jerusalem, aggressively and actively recruits young adults from Reform and Conservative Jewish backgrounds. For Jewish novices like Carter, Aish's initial lure is its Discovery Seminar which packs in facts, uncovers hidden codes in the Torah, and presses thousands of years into the "seven wonders of Jewish history." As its promotional video claims: "We take them on a roller coaster ride through Judaism and they want to get right back on."

Rabbi Stuart Schwartz, who heads Aish's Essentials Program for beginners, says that "our agenda is not to make people Orthodox. It's about increasing Jewish pride." But in reality, Aish operates with a mission of converting Secular

Jews to be strictly observant of Jewish law. Students are taught that God gave the Torah to the Jewish People so they would know how to behave as spiritual beings, and to facilitate their control and suppression of physical desires. By obtaining perfection in Torah, this will assure them everlasting joy and happiness in life. [This makes no sense to me. What about the Observant Jews who witnessed and endured the horrors of the Holocaust? Whatever!] In their courses, Aish teaches that Reform, Conservative, Reconstructionist, and even Modern Orthodoxy are considered cop-outs because they don't strictly follow Torah law. Flexibility is not part of their belief system.

New recruits seem to feel a yearning to connect to their Jewish past and particularly to the Aish family. There is pressure to stay at the yeshiva by the rabbis because they know that if recruits return to their old lives, they are likely not to continue learning. Further, students have the pressure of just being surrounded by all these guys who have been at Aish for years, praying all the time, saying blessings when they eat and after they go to the bathroom, and the newcomers feel like they're not doing enough. They want to join the bandwagon. Immersion in this environment is very effective in leading new recruits to start living a Jewish life, as evidenced by Carter and multitudes of others.

Aish defends themselves against attacks of being a cult-like institution by emphasizing that they encourage new students to investigate by reading and talking to other rabbis, and they suggest that the newcomers not rush into any decisions about becoming religious. While initially Aish does welcome Jewish recruits of all beliefs, politics, levels of observance, and sexual orientation, ultimately they advocate an ultra-Orthodox perspective. All of the rabbis who work at Aish basically have the same viewpoint about Jewish issues so these young people, who have a limited knowledge of Judaism, are not exposed to differing opinions. Hence, the BT is groomed to become an Aish-type of Orthodox person. But in the final analysis, each new recruit decides for himself whether or not to take the plunge into living an observant life.

Our Initial Reactions

When Carter informed us that he had decided to stay in Israel and study to be an Orthodox rabbi, we were mortified. Is this another whim of his? First he was thinking of going to film school, then law school, next he blew off law school, abandoned the South Beach club scene along with women, and decided to immerse himself in Judaism. I figured that he must be brainwashed or how else could our free-spirited, independent thinking son becoming passionate about a religion that requires subservience to rabbinic authority and adherence to a set of rules and regulations. I looked into the possibility of sending someone to Jerusalem to intervene and save Carter from himself. I had read an article written in June 1998 by a mother who believed that her son had been brainwashed into being an Observant Jew by Aish HaTorah (www.rickross.com). He had become unkempt, stopped listening to music, talked only about Judaism, was emaciated, and had a full-body "skin condition." The family hired Rick Ross, an expert on cults and intervention specialist, to deprogram their son. At first I found the article alarming. Then I realized that Carter was not showing any signs of having lost his persona or being negatively affected by his new-found passion for *Torah*. He's still as gregarious as ever, still loves his techno music, can still dance like a wild man, and still enjoys his liquor. To me it seemed evident that Carter's devotion to religion, seemingly out of the blue moon, was indeed influenced by people at Aish HaTorah. But Carter made the decision to go Hard Core. No one forced him into this decision. Handle it. According to Aish, God gave mankind free will so that he could "enjoy the pleasure of his accomplishment of living a Jewish life. We bear full responsibility for our actions and full credit for the good we do. We are free to choose between good and evil. This is what makes the choice of good a true accomplishment." [Whatever!]

We were sad about Carter's metamorphosis into a Hard Core Jewish Kid because our child had taken on such a different way of life than ours. It's like the death of a dream for the future we had hoped for our son. Since Barry, Tyler, and I had no interest in becoming Observant Jews, it was going to be a real challenge to have anything in common with our pious and religiously obedient son. Nonetheless, one has to adjust to changes that occur in life. Parents have to let go and have faith in their children to make the right decisions. Carter is thriving and on fire with a passion for Judaism. He's so happy and content. What more does a parent want for their children? Intuitively I realized that keeping our family connected would require lots of flexibility on our part. Once a newly Observant Jew becomes hooked, forget about him or her going "back to normal." It will not happen. Say goodbye to the Carter we used to know. The new Carter believes that achievement in life should focus only on bringing glory and honor to God and sanctifying His Name. [It's been four years since Carter became an Observant Jew and I'm still saying, "How the hell did this happen?" I'll probably be saying that for the rest of my life because Orthodox Judaism is a complete 180° from the way Carter was raised. When he's in town and staying at home in the lap of luxury relative to how he lives in Israel, I wonder if he will wake up one day and say, "What the heck was I thinking?" But that never happens.]

We were rather appalled at Carter for expecting us to support him while he studied Torah fulltime. Being a multi-tasker, it seemed to me that someone should be able to study Torah and perhaps earn a living too. The reality is that no outstanding Torah scholar ever achieved a high level of learning while he was at the same time involved in secular studies. Moreover, the Jewish community wants to foster Torah scholarship in order to assure that Torah scholars will arise that will be able to teach Torah and render rulings on questions of Jewish law. Since the only way to realize such a goal is by allowing students to dedicate themselves to Torah study on a fulltime basis, it's considered a mitzvah to support a Torah scholar. Carter informed us that by enabling him to study Torah, we earn credit for it in the World To Come (heaven). It turns out that the Jewish People believe that enabling another person to do a mitzvah shows more of a selfless devotion than actually performing the mitzvah. Accordingly, the reward is greater. Such a deal! We like the thought of outsourcing our mitzvahs, so we handed off to Carter and let him earn our rewards in the World To Come while continuing to support him in this world.

Because newly Observant Jews are so anxious to learn everything they can as quickly as possible, they have a tendency to become uni-dimensional and just study day and night. I reminded Carter that while learning Torah will better him as a human being, it doesn't do a thing for his abs. I suggested that he find a way to continue to fit exercise into his life and he has adhered to that. He certainly doesn't devote the kind of time he did in his other life to sculpting his body, but at least he stays in shape.

My heart ached for Carter's unborn children. I feared that they wouldn't have the freedom to be exposed to the multitudes of wonderful sights, experiences, and activities that this incredible world has to offer. They wouldn't be allowed to think independently and be exposed to people who weren't Orthodox Jews. They would have limited knowledge as to how non-observant people live their lives — except when they spend time with me and Barry. Would they get to just be kids and enjoy Mickey Mouse and be carefree? Would they get to experience the thrill of snowboarding down a powder-filled mountain slope? Would they get to play soccer and be on a team? Would they get to act wild at high school football games or attend the prom? Carter's answer to all this was that the life he would be exposing his children to leaves the secular world in the dirt. [Whatever!]

I saw this as an opportunity to learn more about Judaism and my heritage. I realized that casual Jews, due to our ignorance of Jewish laws, traditions, and customs, are sometimes critical or contemptuous of the behavior of Orthodox Jews. I didn't want to act or feel like a bigot and if I could learn and share my knowledge with others, this would certainly be a step in the right direction. Moreover, I found that Observant Jews can be very judgmental toward Secular Jews. If Jews can't get along with one another, how can we expect non-Jews to accept us? I was determined to help Jews at all levels of religiosity become more tolerant of one another.

How Life Has Changed Since Carter Went Hard Core

There is much we all can learn from the sense of discovery, freshness, and remarkable dedication that baalei teshuva (BTs, newly Observant Jews) bring to serving God. They get pleasure from passing their knowledge of the beauty of Judaism along to their loved ones in hopes, that perhaps we lost souls will be inspired to get a little closer to our heritage. In the beginning, like most BTs, Carter acted self-righteously and spent hours on the phone with us from Israel parroting what he had learned at Aish, and urging us to become more observant. He was a bit resentful about the shallow Jewish upbringing he received in our care and our indifferent attitude toward Judaism. He knew that he was doing the right thing now and that we weren't. He would tell us that we weren't truly happy now, and that we would find the greatest possible pleasure and happiness by becoming observant. We told him how lucky he was that he was born into our family because we believe in "different strokes for different folks" and "do your own thing," but most importantly, do not impose your beliefs on us. Eventually he learned to accept the reality of the situation and deal with us at our present level of religious observance. Hey, even though we don't observe Torah law, we're still good people. Carter is extremely grateful for our ability to handle the shock of his metamorphosis, our open-mindedness, our willingness to finance his Torah study, and our pursuit of Jewish knowledge so we can stay close to him. This all reinforced the fact that we are a supportive family with loving ties and unconditional acceptance of each other. The mutual respect and love has made Carter's transition far smoother than it could have been.

It is a fortunate development when a BT is able to relate happily and harmoniously with his/her non-Torah-observant relatives. Obviously, this is not always the case. Parents have a choice of either accepting their offspring's new way of life with their love and support, or rejecting the BTs lifestyle and losing the connection with their child. The BT may be the only Torah-true Jew in his/her entire extended family. There is often very little support from family members. Sometimes there is open hostility or antipathy on the part of their Secular Jewish relatives, or at best, a resigned acceptance of the BTs particular brand of "fundamentalism." Many parents of young adult BTs are bewildered by their alien offspring who seem to be rejecting their upbringing. Families have been torn apart and relationships have been strained, if not destroyed. Even parents who strongly identify with Judaism and belong to Reform, Conservative, and Modern Orthodox branches of the religion are wary of the trappings of Orthodox Judaism.

Rabbi Moshe Rothchild, program director at Manhattan Jewish Experience, a New York City outreach organization, says that parents of BTs generally fall into four distinct categories in their reaction to their children's decision to become Orthodox. "In about 10 percent of cases, parents will consider increasing their observance," Rothchild says. "Other parents are supportive of their children's decision, yet not willing to change their own lifestyle. Still other parents are very neutral. They say, 'If this way of life makes you happy, then we're happy.' In the fourth group are the parents who react hostilely to their children's decisions to become observant, often because they see Orthodoxy as cult-like." One BT with whom Rabbi Rothchild worked reported that her father said to her, "I would rather you were a heroin addict than a religious Jew."

The good news is that Barry and I have become better people since Carter went Hard Core. Carter taught us about the Jewish concept called *loshon hora* that means "evil tongue." It's about watching what you say and who you say it to. We all know that it's not nice to say derogatory things about others, but just being reminded that this is a halachic prohibition helps me hold my tongue. When Carter first told me about loshon hora, I was bummed out. How can the Jewish People take my smut away? Can't I gossip about things I see in People Magazine or in the gossip column of the newspaper? That's so fun, but c'est la vie. The Jewish People want us to be sober and serious and passing smut around is improper.

Carter encouraged us to add a little more Judaism to our lives because it would enhance our closeness to God. He told us that good things will happen to us as a result. What did we have to lose? In Judaism, it's not all or nothing. "Even one moment of consciously refraining from doing *melacha* (a prohibited activity) on Shabbat is a powerful opportunity to get in touch with yourself and God." (aish.com) Barry and I decided to start lighting candles on Friday nights and saying the Sabbath blessings along with the Shema in Hebrew and English. When I light the candles, we are ushering in the Sabbath and I can ask God to protect our family. The only problem we have with this mitzvah is the mandate that the candles are to be lit 18 minutes before sundown. When it's convenient or possible, we light the candles at the "right" time but when it's not, we light the candles when we can. From a halachic point-of-view, we're committing a sin by not lighting candles at the proper time. The Hard Cores believe that if you can't light the candles at the right time, it is better to not light them at all. But intuitively I believe that it has got to be better for unaffiliated Jews like us to even be thinking about God or remembering that we're Jewish, even if it's not 18 minutes before sundown. How can that be bad?

We found out that Barry is not considered Jewish by Observant Jews because his mother wasn't Jewish and she didn't have an Orthodox conversion to Judaism. Who knew that a "Schwartz" could be a non-Jew? That's like someone with the last name of Hernandez not being Hispanic. Jewish law is very clear that only those born from a Jewish mother or who have an Orthodox conversion are truly Jewish. One can have led Jews to the gas chambers in Auschwitz and if his mother was Jewish, then the murderer is Jewish. The person doesn't even have to consider himself Jewish to be Jewish because Jewish law determines whether or not one is Jewish. Although Barry was raised Jewish, always thought of himself as Jewish, had a Bar Mitzvah, and his father was Jewish, none of that is relevant to the Hard Cores. While

Reform Jews believe in patrilineal descent, Orthodox Jews follow the Torah which only accepts matrilineal descent. When Carter informed me that Barry wasn't Jewish, my reply was, "Well, no wonder he can fix things. If he was Jewish, he probably couldn't because Jewish men are notoriously inept in that department." Carter then informed us that our marriage was null and void since Torah law does not recognize civil or common law marriage as a union of two people if both partners are not Jewish. According to the Jewish People, Barry and I have been shacking up illicitly for 35 years. Barry asked Carter if the fact that our marriage is not acknowledged by Jewish law makes him and Tyler bastards. It turns out that even though the Hard Cores do not acknowledge our marriage as being official, our children are not considered bastards *(mamzerim,* in Hebrew*)*. Thank goodness for small favors. Nonetheless, Carter desperately wants his dad to convert to Orthodox Judaism so that Barry can be considered an authentic Jew. But in order for a conversion to be valid, Barry would have to accept all the laws of the Torah. Otherwise the conversion is considered worthless. This means not working, driving or watching TV on Shabbat; keeping kosher at home and away; and much, much more. Another requirement of conversion is for the person to be going through the process for themselves. Barry would be doing it for Carter and that is not acceptable. Barry and I are sincere, ethical, and well-meaning individuals who are trying to make the world a better place in which to live. However, we aren't interested in getting bogged down with Jewish rituals and traditions. Torah-true Judaism is not for everyone.

Now we know what the Torah requires of Carter regarding honoring his parents. We don't hesitate to remind him of this halacha when necessary. [Adapted from "Love Your Neighbor" by Rabbi Zelig Pliskin at Aish HaTorah] Children are supposed to honor their parents by treating them as distinguished, even if they are not. They are supposed to speak to their parents in a soft and pleasant tone and not be disrespectful. The Talmud states that distressing someone with words is worse than cheating them financially. Taking someone's dignity and happiness is worse than taking their money. Children are instructed to treat their parents respectfully by addressing them always as "Mom" or "Dad" or "Mother" or "Father." Calling their parents by their first names is considered disrespectful, as is disturbing their sleep, and sitting in their usual place — whether at home or in the synagogue or another public setting.

While Carter ultimately wants to live in the U.S., it's easier for him to acquire all the Jewish knowledge in Israel that he needs to become an Orthodox rabbi. Carter didn't have any role models while he was growing up who passed on the traditions and principles of Judaism to him. He was like John Locke's blank slate when he got to Aish HaTorah. There are a few yeshivas in the United States that cater to young men who grew up with no Torah learning and minimal *yiddishkeit* (Jewishness), but it's more conducive to keeping God top-of-mind in Israel. There he is surrounded by people who support the same beliefs as him and understand and value his spiritual transformation. More importantly, he is insulated from most of the negative influences of our society, which does not encourage or facilitate dedication to Torah and mitzvot and sacrifices made toward that goal. To the Jewish People, the very soil of Israel is different from that of any other spot on this globe. The Talmud indicates that the land itself is so holy that merely walking in it can gain you a place in the World To Come. Its very air is said to make wise those who pursue knowledge.

The training required to become an Orthodox rabbi is extremely rigorous. Starting out at Aish HaTorah with no yeshiva experience, Carter had to first learn Aramaic, the language in which the Talmud is written. He also had to learn Hebrew, the language spoken in Israel. When Carter receives his rabbinic ordination (*smicha pronounced SMEEK-ha)*, he will be considered a Torah expert and authorized to give advice or judgment in Jewish law. Carter now attends classes at the Mirrer Yeshiva in Jerusalem in the morning, and then studies at Aish in the afternoon. Neither yeshiva has a specific curriculum that details the number of years it will take for him to obtain rabbinic ordination. Timing all depends on how long it takes Carter to become a Torah scholar. One day when we least expect it, he'll be done. Then he wants to come back to Miami and be involved in some Jewish leadership role, but what exactly he'll do and how he'll make a living doing it is another story. That's not real important to the Hard Core Jewish People because Torah rules and God will take care of them somehow. Carter has the potential to be a great Jewish leader who understands the American Jewish scene because he's been on both the secular and observant sides and graduated from the number four college in the U.S. He's very intelligent and speaks in a manner that Secular Jews can understand. He may have more success than others in involving Jews in their Jewish heritage. Time will tell.

There is a dearth of great rabbis in the U.S. because most of them end up going back to Israel. It is much less expensive for them to live there because of socialized medicine and yeshiva education for their children is subsidized. They can isolate and insulate themselves from the broader community and place absolute adherence to religious laws and customs above all other goals. Moreover, no one in Israel thinks that it's strange that men and women in our day and age will willingly forgo opportunities to enjoy the material rewards that come with fulltime employment in favor of lives of Torah study and observance. In Israel they regard Torah study much like most of us regard medical research – as something so worthy in its own right that it is worth pursuing, even if it brings economic disadvantage. ·

Life has also changed in the political arena. Our family has always been Democrats, but Carter voted for Bush in 2004. It's not so much that Bush is a Republican but rather he was the most advantageous candidate for Jewish issues. Orthodox Jews are extremely conservative, both religiously and politically. Results released July 2005 from a poll by Yeshiva University found that Orthodox and non-Orthodox Jews held diametrically opposite views on a host of national security issues related to the Middle East conflict. Over half of the Orthodox respondents (59%) said they think the U.S.

and Israel are more secure because of the Iraq War, while 58% of Conservative Jews and 70% of Reform Jews indicated that the countries were less safe as a result of the Iraq War. Moreover, 80% of Orthodox Jews vs. 34% of Conservative Jews and 30% of Reform Jews have a favorable view of George W. Bush. On Israel's scheduled pullout from Gaza, 56% of Orthodox Jews reported opposing the plan, while two-thirds (66%) of Conservative Jews and nearly three out of every four (72%) Reform Jews said they support it. Even now, with quantitative evidence to prove that Sharon's decision to build the separation fence and his unilateral withdrawal from Gaza have reduced Palestinian terror attacks by 90%, the Jewish People will not admit the success of his strategy and how it has directly led to Israel's improved economy. In Gaza, there were 8,000 Jews and 1.4 million Palestinians and no Jewish religious and historical significance there. The Jews could not hold their own without the Israeli army and the place wasn't worth it. By giving up territory in which Jews were the clear minority, Israelis are more secure. But the ultra-Orthodox are not into reality; they do not want to give up one iota of land, no matter what the consequences are. They prefer being stubborn and are not interested in making compromises or peace because they assume that peace is not possible with an Arab population ideologically bent upon wiping out every Jew. From a truly Jewish viewpoint, informed by Jewish ideals and Jewish texts, the single most important part of Jewish security is the practice and study of Torah. While Jewish tradition mandates the employment of conventional means, like armies and arsenals, for maintaining the security of Jews, it has been the Jewish conviction for millennia that the true safety of the Jewish People derives, in the end, from dedication to the values, laws, and study of the Torah.

A Guide for Sharing Space with an Observant Jew

If you refuse to become an Orthodox Jew but still want to continue to have a relationship with your newly observant loved one, you need to become familiar with some of the basic *halacha* (Jewish law) requirements so that you can share space. Due to all of the stringent lifestyle regulations of Orthodoxy, it is usually the parents who end up accommodating their children. Whether or not we agree with their decision to become religious is irrelevant – one needs to create an environment in which the BT (newly Observant Jew) can adhere to halacha or forget about them coming home for a visit.

Controlling Over-Zealousness

[Xanax-mode alert] When they first turn Hard Core, BTs are so focused on staying Torah-true that they are fairly inflexible to any halachic leniency. They are far less likely than those raised in the Orthodox community to tolerate deviations from Torah standards, or to excuse those deviations as just the way things are. You can make Alice B. Toklas kosher brownies (they include marijuana as an ingredient for those of you who didn't grow up in the 60's) to mellow your BT out or verbally intimidate him like I did. "Carter, I don't know who this *Hashem*-person is who wants my kid to sit and read the Torah instead of swimming with me when you're finally home for a visit." The rabbis at Aish encourage BTs to not waste a minute of time nor be seduced by the pleasures of the world. But the pleasures of the world can be a lot of fun and are necessary so that one doesn't become uni-dimensional. Family time has got to be a priority. Parents need to remind their passionately-Jewish loved one that halachically-speaking, he/she is allowed to relax, as long as it is purposeful and directed. It's a challenge but don't be intimidated. BTs are so turned on by Judaism that nothing that gives only physical pleasure is considered worthwhile to them. Carter is now a person who doesn't care about the Miami Dolphins or watching any football games because fleeting pleasure or pain doesn't begin to compare to the joy of learning Torah and feeling close to God. [Whatever!]

Create a Kosher Portion of Your Kitchen

Relax and go into Xanax-mode. It can be a major pain-in-the-neck to accommodate a kosher houseguest, but it's doable. I've been asked to do much more difficult things in my lifetime. Just keep those pills handy. In order for Carter to be able to stay at our house, a top priority was making a portion of our kitchen kosher. Carter can't use any of our stuff because it's contaminated with *traif* (pronounced trayf; non-kosher food). We identified one overhead three-shelved cabinet and two good-sized drawers to officially declare as "Kosher Only." I've always liked the quote that if something only requires writing a check, then it's an expense — not a problem. Then I got to go out and buy a complete set of pots and pans, dishes for four, silverware, utensils, and literally everything one would need to eat and cook with at our house. Of course I could have used paper and plastic. I just wanted to make Carter feel truly at home with the real thing. With shelving organizers and containers, everything fit neatly into the allocated space. We lucked-out because Carter is allergic to milk and does not eat dairy. Otherwise we would have had to have a separate set of everything in which to serve and cook dairy products. By the way, separating milk and meat is mentioned in the Torah but there is no explanation as to why this is necessary. Observant Jews follow this halacha because it is the will of God. Take a pill and handle it.

Toiveling [Xanax-mode alert] *Toiveling* (TOY-vel-ing) is the immersion into a *mikvah* (a Jewish ritual bath found at most Orthodox synagogues) of nearly all vessels and utensils that have been previously owned or manufactured by non-Jews that will be used for eating. It purifies the utensil from contact with non-Jews and gives the item an additional measure of holiness. [Carter informed us that it was also an option to use a natural body of water for the toiveling, like our canal. Yuck!] Thus, many of those sparkling new items you purchased for your kosher loved one will first have to be toiveled before you can use them. Make your loved one handle the toiveling so he/she gets to directly experience the hassles involved in his/her lifestyle change. Moreover, the Hard Core Jewish Person can feel comfortable knowing that the toilveling was done properly because prayers also need to be said during the immersion of most utensils. After the toiveling, each of the items needs to be washed again in your kitchen sink with kosher soap and water and dried with a non-traif dish towel.

Microwave: We kasher (rhymes with washer and means 'to make kosher') the microwave by placing a paper bowl with water inside and cooking it for 5 minutes so it reaches a rolling boil. Why does the bowl have to be paper you ask? [Warning: Go into Xanax-mode!] Because before the microwave is kashered, a kosher dish can't be put inside because it wouldn't be kosher anymore, and we also can't use a traif dish because that would contaminate the water.

Oven – If you don't have a self-cleaning oven, get one. The self-cleaning process takes care of making the oven kosher.

Stovetop – Clean the burners with a wet cloth and then turn them on high for a few minutes. That burns off any non-kosher cooties that might have remained behind.

Barbeque – Scrape off any loose food and then turn it on for 10 minutes and it's kashered. Don't forget to toivel any barbeque utensils that were used on your previously non-kosher barbeque. First you need to clean them thoroughly to de-contaminate them and then comes the toiveling.

Dishwasher – It can't really be kashered unless you can remove and replace all of the racks. Instead, buy a plastic dish drainer and let the Hard Core Jewish Person do his/her dishes. You'll need special dish towels for drying the kosher dishes, and separate ones for meat and dairy unless you can launder them in between meat and dairy usage.

<u>Sink</u> – Keep a kosher sponge, kosher scrub pad, kosher soap, ceramic or plastic kosher mug by the sink so the BT can wash his/her hands and say a prayer before meals that involve eating bread. Inside the sink you will need a protector that sits on the floor and prevents the kosher dishes from getting contaminated by your traif sink. You'll need a separate rack for meat and dairy.

<u>Spices and Staples</u> – They have to have an OU or Star K certification. Wait for the Hard Core Jewish Person to go grocery shopping with you if possible.

<u>Outsource</u> - Find a great kosher deli and grocery store so you can fill your house with goodies that will make your loved one feel welcome. Also find out the location of kosher restaurants.

Ditch the Observant One On Friday Night (Shabbat)

If at all possible, have your BT sleep out on Friday night so he/she can be in reasonable walking distance to a synagogue (since driving isn't allowed) and so you don't have to be burdened with the Shabbat halacha, which is extensive. For example:

- If you'll need to use your stove on the Sabbath, it has to be turned on before sundown on Friday and left on until after sundown on Saturday.

- Any lights that you need to use have to be turned on Friday before sundown and left on until after sundown on Saturday. It's a good idea to cover the switch with tape so no one accidentally commits heresy.

- One of the 39 primary Shabbat restrictions is not tearing. This means that any toilet paper and dental floss for you and guests that will be needed on the Sabbath must be torn in advance of the Sabbath. Dental floss can only be used on the Sabbath by those whose gums don't bleed when they floss.

- Your doorbell cannot be used. [That's one of the easy requirements.]

- The refrigerator light cannot come on when the refrigerator is open. Same is true for the oven light and the burglar alarm lights that come on when the door is opened.

- Needless to say, we're not supposed to turn on and off any electrical appliances. The one time Carter was home for Shabbat, Barry and I retreated to our master bedroom where we were free to get on our treadmill or watch television.

Skip Passover Visits Home (The Cover Picture Story)

Do not invite your loved one home for Passover. As if being kosher wasn't difficult enough, Passover is a minefield of rules and regulations unto itself. Even the Hard Core Jewish People leave their homes and stay in hotels or on cruise ships over Passover because the regulations are overwhelming.

The picture on the cover of this book was taken on April 28, 2005 after our family nearly fell apart and then came together again. It was near the end of Passover when Tyler and Carter were in town for the holiday. It was the first time in two years the four of us had been together, and the first time in two years that the brothers had been face-to-face. It had been three years and three months since Carter went Hard Core. We had survived Passover with Carter two years earlier and like childbirth, the pain and suffering had dissipated so I figured we would try it again. I just so much wanted the four of us to unite that I went with my heart and not my brain. We nearly pulled if off, even though everyday Carter would make comments to the three of us for violating some Passover law. But he also regularly expressed his appreciation to us for going to the trouble of getting the four of us together for Passover. I, who never cooks when the boys aren't in town, planned Kosher for Passover menus and cooked nearly everyday. *[What won't we do for our precious children?]*

Passover 2005 began on a Saturday night one hour after sundown. Orthodox Jewish women had to do all of their

Passover preparation prior to the Sabbath. On the Sabbath, one can clean dishes, prepare food, and generally slave away only on things that will be used on the Sabbath. If it is going to be used on an occasion after the Sabbath, it will have to wait until Shabbat is over. Discussion over! The Sabbath is sacred.

For two days following the first Seder, Hard Core Jewish People treat those days like the Sabbath and are restricted in the same ways. We had our stove and oven on from Friday evening until Monday at sundown along with all of the lights inside and outside the house. My mind had a bit of trouble getting used to all the lights in the house being on. When do we ever waste electricity? Barry had to fix the refrigerator so the light wouldn't come on when anyone opened it. We couldn't use the dispensers on the refrigerator door for ice because we would be activating power. My girlfriend from elementary school was joining us for the Seder [even though she was still traumatized from the one she attended at our house two years previously] and would be spending the night. I asked Carter, "What if Maxine needs the light off in order to sleep?" He said that Barry could turn the light off if Maxine requested it since Barry isn't Jewish [because his mother wasn't Jewish]. So what if a goy (non-Jew) violates a Jewish mitzvah!

On the fourth day of Passover, our family was planning on having lunch on the patio and spending the afternoon together. Tyler had a yen for a fresh salad. The kosher rules for cleaning vegetables are so oppressive that Tyler and I decided to go to Wild Oats Supermarket and pick up an organic salad rather than preparing one at home. At the store, Tyler inadvertently put non-kosher for Passover salad dressing on his salad, and we both discussed how he would take it around back to the patio and not bring it in the house when we got home. But by the time we got home and I pulled into the garage, that thought had left our minds. Instead of going around back, Tyler walked into the house and put his salad down in the family room while he went back into the kitchen to get a fork. For those of you who don't know, having non-kosher for Passover food in one's house during Passover is worthy of being stoned to death or something equally unpleasant. Carter walked into the family room, spotted the salad on the coffee table, and went ballistic. He shrieked at us and abruptly grabbed the salad and brought it outside in a gruff and rough manner. That unnecessary overreaction put Tyler over the edge. Tyler said that he was through with Carter because the person who replaced Carter was a Torah-law obsessed person and he no longer recognized him. That couldn't be his brother.

I started crying because I saw this crisis as the beginning of the end of our family unit. Tears kept pouring down my cheeks. My parents both died young from cancer, my younger sister hates me, and now our family was dissolving because of some Hard Core Jewish Kid who prioritized Torah law over being civil. I said: "Carter, do you have to treat an unintentional violation of God's law as if it is worthy of capital punishment? Anyway, we did the violation — not you. Why would God blame it on you? If we called Rabbi

Becker at Young Israel (Carter's Orthodox rabbi in Miami) and told him what was transpiring here, would he say, 'Torah rules. The heck with family?' I don't think so."

Carter, who had been sitting at the patio table with me and Barry while Tyler sat on the opposite side of the patio eating his salad, got up and started punching the air because he was so disgusted with his behavior. In his passion to be Torah-true, Carter had nearly alienated his brother. Tyler and Carter have always been close, but this Hard Core Judaism was driving a stake between them. Carter started crying because he realized how out-of-control he had been and apologized profusely to all of us. Next thing we knew, he went into the house, took off his kippa (yarmulke), put on a baseball cap and a bathing suit, then came back to the patio and jumped into the pool. Tyler joined him and in a matter of minutes, the boys became brothers again and our family was saved.

I started writing this book that night. Our family had survived a major crisis and I felt compelled to help others keep their families together when one of the members becomes fanatically observant. I had learned so much about Judaism since Carter's spiritual transformation, and now I felt like Hashem wanted me to share my knowledge with the world. That was my mission. The next day I told Carter I was writing a book and would be doing way more kiruv (KEE-roove or bringing unaffiliated Jews closer to Judaism) than his yeshiva and Orthodox Jews could ever hope to do. Since ninety percent of Jews are not Orthodox, I have more of a chance of being able to communicate meaningfully to them than do the Hard Core Jewish People.

Keeping Kosher

Why do Torah-adherent Jews observe the laws of Kashrut (KASH-root, Jewish dietary laws)? Because God commanded them to, and by fulfilling this commandment, they connect to God. There is no need for any other reason. Eating kosher is part of the Covenant that Torah-true Jews take seriously. They show their reverence to God by following these laws even though they do not know the reason. It elevates the simple act of eating into a religious ritual. Moreover, Kashrut laws also have to do with ensuring that Jews maintain a social distance from their neighbors. The reason has to do with the threat of intermarriage. If Jews keep kosher – eating only certain foods prepared in certain ways in certain kitchens – their ability to socialize with their non-Jewish and non-observant neighbors and friends, is limited. The likelihood of their sons and daughters marrying outside their faith will be that much more reduced.

Keeping kosher can be very time consuming and boring. For example, the thoroughness required for cleaning fresh vegetables is enough to drive most of us to the funny farm. I would need to be smoking Jamaican ganja or on LSD in order to get through it. Bless the hearts of any Hard Core Jewish Women who can feel inspired and closer to God when performing this task. Here are some examples of how to clean vegetables from <u>Is It Kosher?</u> by Rabbi E. Eidlitz.

<u>Artichokes</u>: Each leaf down to the heart of the plant must be individually inspected.

<u>Asparagus & Broccoli</u>: Soak florets in lukewarm water in a lightly colored bowl. Run finger through the florets and agitate them in the water by holding onto the stem. Inspect the water. If insects are present, empty the water and repeat this procedure until the water is insect-free. Rinse the vegetable before using.

<u>Cabbage and Lettuce</u>: Some hold that merely removing the loose, outer leaves allows one to use the entire vegetable without further inspection, if the vegetable is U.S. grown. Nevertheless, it is still preferable to inspect three additional inner leaves and flush the remaining leaves in running water. There is another view that holds that all leaves must be soaked in a vinegar solution and then individually inspected.

Three Categories of Kosher Food

<u>Meat</u> includes the meat or bones of mammals and fowl, soups or gravies made with them, and any food containing even a small quantity of the above. <u>Dairy</u> includes the milk of any kosher animal, all milk products made with it (cream, butter, cheese, etc), and any food containing even a small

quantity of the above. Meat and Dairy are never combined. Separate utensils and dishes are used for each, and a waiting period is observed between eating them. <u>Pareve</u> (pronounced parve) foods are neither "meat" nor "dairy" and they include no milk products. Fish and eggs are pareve, as are all fruits, vegetables and grains. Pareve foods can be mixed with and eaten together with either meat or dairy.

Checking Out the Scene in Israel

In December 2002, I decided to make the trek to Israel and check out the scene there. I wanted to know how safe my kid really was and to meet the people who convinced Carter to go Hard Core. Since Israel is not a place we think of as a vacation destination, Barry stayed home and minded the fort and off I went for a one week trip. [Barry ultimately went on his own solo trip there in December 2004.]

It was a little scary the first time I ever saw *tefillin* which was on the El Al flight to Tel Aviv. *Tefillin* are two small black boxes with black straps attached to them. Jewish men are required to place one box on their head and tie the other one on their arm each weekday morning when they say their morning prayers. The reason that the Hard Cores wear tefillin is based on the V-ahavta portion of the Shema blessing: "And you shall bind them as a sign on your hand, and they shall be for frontlets between your eyes." [I told you they take everything seriously.]

No one had warned me about the tough, emotionally hardened, arrogant, and ruthless characteristics of many Israelis. My first exposure to them was when I tried to collect my luggage at Ben Gurion Airport in Tel Aviv. I had to lunge over people who surrounded the luggage carousel on all sides. Forget about courtesy and human consideration – it's each man for himself. Trying to rationalize their rude behavior, I figured that Israelis are faced with such hardships and tragedies and their lives are so precarious that they have to be mentally tough for the sake of survival. Carter met me with roses and at last I could hug my son again. It had been eleven months since I had seen him. He still looked like Carter – he was wearing a kippa (yarmulke) but otherwise there were no visible telltale signs of his religious devotion.

We took a cab from the airport to my hotel in Jerusalem and the cab driver described the sites I was seeing along the way. Just viewing the countryside and the architecture and learning about the history made me feel more in touch with my Jewishness. It was Friday afternoon, just before the Sabbath was going to begin, so I had the opportunity to see the hustle and bustle of the last minute shoppers in the open-air marketplace. Observant Jews are very obsessive about meeting the requirements of Torah law. On Fridays they rush around like maniacs and get all stressed out in fear that they might be late for the 18 minutes before sundown requirement to light those Sabbath candles and go into Shabbat-mode. When Shabbat begins, the tumult of Shabbat preparation ends and a peacefulness overtakes the city. Most stores and restaurants are closed in Jerusalem until an hour after sundown on Saturday. When we got to the hotel, I barely had time to take a quick shower before we had to leave to get to the Western Wall so that Carter could *daven* (pray) in time.

The Western Wall or Kotel is in the midst of the Old City in Jerusalem, directly across from Carter's yeshiva. You can view a live web cam of it on the aish.com website. The

Western Wall is part of the retaining wall of the Temple Mount, which was the site of the First and Second Temples in ancient times. It is the only remnant of the Temple that Jews can touch, pray to, and weep upon. This has made the Western Wall the most hallowed spot in Jewish religious and national consciousness and tradition. The Western Wall at sunset on Shabbat is the Hard Core Jews' version of happy hour. There isn't any liquor there or guys trying to pick up women. Rather, the square is filled with pious people praising Hashem (God) and celebrating the start of Shabbat. Some people stand so close to the wall when rocking back and forth praying that I wondered if anyone ever knocks themselves out by banging their head on the wall. I watched as people said their prayers and then left to have Shabbat dinner. Naturally Carter, passionate newly Observant Jew that he is, prayed for what seemed like hours and by the time we were finally ready to leave, I had been standing in the cold and was chilled. Little did I know then that three days later, I would have an upper respiratory infection and laryngitis. No biggie – one has to be tough to hang with the Hard Core Jewish People.

As inhospitable as the people were at Ben Gurion Airport, I found the Jewish People to be incredibly warm and welcoming as they open their homes to friends, acquaintances, and family for Friday night dinner and Saturday lunch. It's common knowledge that the Jewish People are very big on eating in general, but on Shabbat, the importance of food is escalated. Unlike weekday meals, those eaten on Shabbat are not for physical sustenance alone but serve to fulfill the *mitzvah* (obligation) of Sabbath joy. It is also a mitzvah to eat three Shabbat meals: Friday evening, Saturday lunch, and late afternoon. For the third meal which takes place shortly before the end of Shabbat, Carter and I hosted a buffet for a bunch of the guys who he studied with at his yeshiva. I wanted to meet these people and hear their stories of how they made their way to Israel and Observant Judaism.

Lo and behold, Carter's Aish HaTorah peers entered the room and they all looked like regular people. These guys didn't look like weirdos – not all of them had beards and those that did kept them trimmed and neat. Unlike the Hassidim who wear black hats and black wool coats even in the summer, these guys are more subtle about displaying their Jewishness. They come from all walks of life and many different countries. The universal ingredient that landed them at Aish HaTorah was a search for the inner meaning of life and existence. They opted for the high road and decided to live their lives according to God. I had them go around the table and tell me their story of how they ended up at Aish HaTorah. Most of them hadn't heard each other's stories before, and so all of us were enlightened with these fascinating tales that are worthy of being made into a movie. Many of the men had to defy parents and society to make their way to the Holy Land. Unlike Carter, whose decision to study Torah in Israel was being subsidized by his benefactors (Barry and me), most of the guys had used their own money to get to where they were. [Barry and I are probably not the best people to ask for child-rearing advice, considering what softies we are.]

During my Israel visit, I had the honor of having a meeting with Rabbi Noah Weinberg, the rosh yeshiva (dean / head honcho) and founder of Aish HaTorah. The guy looks like Abraham and one feels humbled in his presence because of his eminence and success with *kiruv* (Jewish outreach, i.e., making people more Jewish). Rabbi Weinberg asked me how we raised Carter because he was a champion yeshiva student. Carter had all the ingredients to rise to the top and was already well on his way. I was flabbergasted that someone was interested in our child-rearing techniques since all of our friends flash the anti-vampire sign when they see us coming. I told the rabbi that we encouraged Carter to think for himself, to have an open-mind, and explore all the possibilities the world has to offer. I suggested to the rabbi that while I realized that studying Torah was where it's at, it seemed wasteful that these yeshiva guys are warehoused studying Torah far away from any anti-Semitism. "I think that every student here should be required to reach out to at least one person every single day, and have a positive impact in addition to their studying Torah. With all due respect, there's so much anti-Semitism out there, even that of uneducated Jews toward Orthodox Jews, and the world doesn't stand still while these guys sit inside all day studying Torah." The rabbi nodded his head and agreed with me, but as far as actions go, nothing came of that conversation.

My trip to Israel coincided with a fast day (from dawn to dusk) called the Tenth of Tevet. This observance is historically tied in with events surrounding the destruction of the First Ancient Temple. The purpose of the fast is not the commemoration of an historical event, but rather to heighten their awareness of the evil deeds of their ancestors and their own evil deeds and repent. The Tenth of Tevet is viewed as such a severe and important fast day that it is observed even if it falls on a Friday. All other fast days are arranged by calendar adjustments as to never fall on a Friday so as not to interfere with Shabbat preparations. I ended up taking a tour of the Western Wall tunnel that day. In front of the Western Wall of the Temple Mount is an incredible labyrinth of tunnels, arches, and passageways that had remained untouched for centuries. Through extensive archaeological excavations during the last few decades culminating in the explosive opening of an exit in the autumn of 1996, this is now a "must see" site in Jerusalem. Inside the tunnel, I saw women sitting and crying as they *davened* (prayed) against the tunnel walls. You have to understand that the Jews take the destruction of the Temple very seriously. They want to repent and atone for all the bad things done by Jews in days gone by as well as now. My first reaction was that sitting and crying and praying in the tunnel is something to do and at least it keeps them out of the mall. But the sobbing has got to be exhausting. In the Western Wall square when we came out of the tunnel, it was packed with guys wailing and praying aloud. I found a comfortable seat and read my book until Carter came and found me. Different strokes for different folks.

Carter and I had sushi at the David Citadel Hotel one night with Rabbi Motty Burger, a fabulous Aish rabbi. I almost ruined Motty's life that night because after two sakis, I accidentally reached over and touched him on the shoulder when I was talking. I told you we're a touchy-feely family. Anyway, we all just laughed and I'm assuming that God forgave me for my minor transgression. Motty and Carter walked me back to my hotel after dinner and then proceeded to the Old City. I heard guests in the room next to mine cheering for the Dolphins. I turned on my television and there was a great Dolphins game happening. [That's when they were still good.] I called Carter on his cell to tell him to turn on the game. I had forgotten that they don't have TVs in yeshivas and even if they did, TV doesn't give an iota of the pleasure that paying homage to Hashem does. Caring about the Dolphins gives one fleeting pleasure or displeasure, depending upon how they're playing. Worshipping Hashem, on the other hand, leads to a lasting satisfaction that only gets stronger over time. Silly goose that I am, I informed Carter about the game and he told me he was in the middle of doing other things. I said, "Let me speak to the authorities. My kid no longer cares about the Dolphins." That's not really true because Carter likes Barry to keep him up-to-speed with what's happening in sports. He's just not interested in utilizing his time anymore in such a frivolous manner as watching a football game. Getting closer to God is his priority. [Whatever!]

The entire time I was in the Old City, I felt safe and not fearful of my life. At least I had peace-of-mind knowing that

Carter's life wasn't in danger anymore than the rest of our lives are with regard to terrorism. However, Israel isn't my kind of place. The people are extremely aggressive and from the minute one's feet touch the ground at Ben Gurion airport, you have to be "on." Just crossing a street at a crosswalk is a challenge because pedestrians don't seem to have the right-of-way in Israel. Moreover, because of the praying requirements of Orthodox Jews and Carter's schedule, I found myself waiting around a lot which is boring and made me feel unproductive. Finally, the topography of Israel isn't appealing to me. Rather than religious sights, deserts, and beaches on the Mediterranean or Dead Sea, I prefer snow, beautiful mountains, and oceans. While it was nice experiencing Israel and making our son very happy, I was jubilant when my feet touched U.S. soil.

Looking for Love

The Matchmaker and the Babe

After Carter's third year in Israel, the rabbis at Aish HaTorah decided that he had reached the appropriate level of emotional maturity and Torah knowledge necessary to handle the obligations, responsibilities, and duties of marriage. This meant that it was time to line up a matchmaker to "find him a match, catch him a catch." A lot of thought, insight, and investigation go into the process of bringing two people of the opposite sex together. The matchmaker is an objective and trained professional who learns everything about her clients including their assets, liabilities, the kind of qualities they are looking for in a mate, their Jewish lineage, religious behavior, and personal lives, and then tries to match them up with an appropriate person. It's a screening process. She's not arranging a marriage but rather is in pursuit of setting up a meeting of two individuals (called a *shidduch*) who are seemingly compatible. Once the couple meets, they determine on their own if the other person is the right fit for them.

Aish HaTorah commissioned a matchmaker to find suitable and appropriate women for their champion yeshiva student to meet. A Torah scholar like Carter doesn't have time to futz around with dating women who don't satisfy his mandatory requirements of being someone attractive who would support his religious goals, create a beautiful home environment, and make him an even better person than he is alone. He wasn't looking to date for the sake of dating. He was looking for his match made in heaven. Over the course of around a year-and-a-half, he ended up going out with a total of five women, none of whom he felt any chemistry. Then he met Naomi Rosenthal, and there was an immediate connection.

Naomi was on a two-and-a-half week vacation in Israel visiting friends and relatives, during which time she coincidentally contacted Carter's matchmaker in hopes of finding someone to love. Naomi had gone out with numerous guys over the years and had not found any of them appealing. Unlike many Observant Jewish women who marry very young, Naomi was in college for seven years obtaining a joint B.S. and Optometry degree from SUNY State College of Optometry. She was looking for a mate with a high level of commitment to and knowledge of Torah as well as having secular knowledge. She thought something was wrong with her because most of the men she met lacked qualities that would earn her respect. Naomi's mom, Carol, was thinking that her daughter was too picky, because how could all of these guys be the wrong one? They had both forgotten that the most important thing is to have *emunah* or faith in God. It is He who plans the match and puts the souls together so they can merge as one. The saying "a match made in heaven" is consistent with the Talmudic dictum that 40 days before a male child is born, a heavenly proclamation declares, "the daughter of so-and-so is destined for this person." Like Carter, Naomi had to be patient and wait for her *beshert* (soul mate).

After two in-depth telephone conversations and a face-to-face meeting with Naomi, the matchmaker was certain that Naomi and Carter were meant to be. She first told Naomi about Carter, and Naomi was interested in meeting him. Then she called Carter at 4pm on Thursday, July 28th, three days before Naomi was scheduled to return to New York, and told him about Naomi. He too was interested in a meeting, so the fix-up agent suggested that Carter see Naomi before Shabbat the next day. Carter counter-proposed that they waste no time and connect that evening instead. That is exactly what they ended up doing. [What's really sweet is that when I went to Israel to meet Naomi and her folks, Naomi and I were walking around Jerusalem and she showed me the exact spot where she was when her cell phone rang and the matchmaker informed her that she was going out with Carter that night. It gave me goose bumps.]

The protocol for the first meeting is that it be a neutral place (which is not a place of entertainment), and conversation is the main focus. Each side asks questions about the other, and shares their feelings and opinions openly so that the other side can understand their character, their desires, and their direction. There is no touching of the other person allowed – a *shidduch* (meeting) is a hands-free event. The philosophy is that sex before marriage, including hugging and kissing, can cause emotional attachments before the partner has been certified as worthy and appropriate by the mind. After the meeting, the couple is supposed to report back to the matchmaker as to whether they liked each other well enough to continue dating. Typically, Observant Jewish couples date only each other for the duration of their relationship and generally go out for a limited amount of time before deciding to become engaged or end the relationship. This, of course, is primarily a result of their not being able to touch until they're married. Imagine how difficult an undertaking this must be when hormones are in high gear and a couple feels passion.

It turns out that the thing about Naomi that initially captured Carter's interest on their first date was her willingness to call him on something he said about Judaism that she felt was inaccurate. Carter is pretty much an expert on everything, and he can be fairly intimidating at times. Very sweetly and gently, Naomi corrected him on some issue and he was impressed. Carter liked that Naomi had the chutzpa to "shut me down." They each reported back to their mediator that the meeting had gone well and that they were interested in another date. They went out again on Friday before the Sabbath and on Saturday night, after the Sabbath and that's when they both decided that Naomi should cancel her flight home the following day.

Carter and Naomi went out a multitude of times and frequently talked on the phone. The intensity of the relationship enabled each of them to determine whether this person was sincere, stable, authentic, and someone they could relate to, trust, and appreciate. Naomi had every quality that Carter wanted in his wife including being well educated, sophisticated, pretty, having a Jewish heart and soul, possessing a high level of Jewish observance, willing to live in Israel while he studied Torah, and amenable to ultimately living in the U.S. Carter dazzled Naomi by the level of Torah knowledge that he had acquired in only three and a half years and his commitment to Judaism. He was a man that she greatly respected and she also liked his looks. Even Hard Core Jewish People care about aesthetics.

Carter proposed marriage to Naomi three weeks after they met. When it's right, you know it. He was certain that Naomi was the one for him, and I was thrilled that he took time off from Torah study to decide whether he should sprinkle the entrance to the room where he would propose with rose petals or single roses. Carter followed the Orthodox Jewish custom of giving Naomi a bracelet instead of a ring in honor of their engagement. The reason a bracelet is given is that the man and woman cannot touch until they are married, so the groom-to-be would be unable to put the ring on his bride-to-be's finger. Moreover, since the bride is the one who will be wearing the ring for the rest of her life, it makes sense for her to select the one she likes. Needless to say, Naomi was thrilled when Carter popped the question and she was grateful that she passed the matchmaker's suitability test for Aish HaTorah's diamond Torah scholar. Naomi had to meet all sorts of people before God allowed her to find the man of her dreams. Carter and Naomi both thank God for bringing them together. Coincidentally, they were born on the same day and the first letter of their Hebrew names, when put together, means "miracle."

Shortly after they became engaged, Carter and Naomi called me on the telephone. When I spoke to Naomi, I knew from the sound of her voice and the words she was saying that she was deeply in love with Carter. I felt like I was inside her head and sensed exactly what she was feeling. I felt a rapport with her instantly, and was certain that Carter had picked the right woman to settle down with. Moreover, Barry and I would be inheriting a wonderful daughter-in-law.

The Parents Meet

Barry and I were doing rebel yells when Carter informed us that he was going to propose to Naomi. Now we could hand-off our piece of work to the lady of his dreams. Carter proposed on a Friday and the following Thursday, Carol and Stuart (Naomi's folks), Rachel, her sister nearly three years her junior, and I converged in Israel. We had to meet each other and discuss the upcoming wedding. Because of the last-minute nature of the trip, Barry stayed home and I went solo again to Israel. I arrived in Tel Aviv at 9am and was greeted at the airport by Naomi and Carter with roses for me. Then we jumped into a cab and I was whisked away, with all my luggage, to the Tel Aviv Diamond Exchange to buy Naomi a diamond ring. Here's an all points bulletin. If your son is a Torah scholar and becomes engaged to an Orthodox Jewish woman from New York, duck and cover. Being a

Secular Jew, I had no idea of the New York Orthodox Jewish wedding customs so I was blind-sided. I didn't want to make a scene, but I found the whole experience shocking. It appears that because Carter is a Torah scholar, the groom's parents are expected to pay for the ring, assuming they can afford to. I had never heard of such a thing, and it would have been a nice touch if Carter had forewarned me. Oh well. At least it's a mitzvah. Actually Israel is a good place to buy diamonds because it is one of the leading world diamond trading centers in the world for polished and rough diamonds. Security was rather intense at the Diamond Exchange which housed millions of dollars worth of diamonds. Carter had to stay downstairs in the lobby with my luggage because he didn't have a passport with him. It didn't really matter since moneybags (that be me) was the one who had to pay and Naomi is the one who would be selecting the diamond. She chose a beautiful diamond of topnotch color and clarity, and I was glad for her to have it. Naomi is a very special woman, one of the kindest people I have ever met, and this would be a lifetime (hopefully) token of Carter's love for her.

When we finally got to Jerusalem, about a 45-minute drive from Tel Aviv, I checked into the hotel and took my time unpacking and showering. I was still going strong since arriving in Israel, while Naomi's parents had napped all afternoon. We were meeting for dinner and this would be the first time they laid eyes on Carter. I was running late but figured this would be okay with the Rosenthal's since it would give them time to schmooze with Carter before I got there. Carter called me at my hotel from a taxi on his way to the restaurant and reported that he had just noticed a giant hole in his pants. This was getting to be like a sitcom. Fortunately no one noticed the rip. [Carol later told me that Carter was very different in appearance than all of the men Naomi had dated previously. They were pleasantly surprised to see that he didn't arrive wearing a black hat or have a beard but rather was this good-looking GQ kind-of-guy.]

Carol and Stuart are Modern Orthodox Jews who have always lived in Queens, New York. Stuart is the co-president of their synagogue and they observe the Sabbath and keep kosher. They are very down-to-earth and good-hearted, and the most tolerant and accepting people I've ever met. It's so easy to like them. They had no problem with Carter's parents being secular. Their daughter was madly in love with Carter, and Carol and Stuart viewed him as the Messiah. This was the highlight of their lives. For years they had been saving money for their daughters' weddings as well as to help them after they were married. Rachel had been married three years previously. Now, at long last, their first-born daughter had found the perfect mate. You have to realize that being married is of imminent importance to Jewish women. Many young women begin their search upon graduation from high school. Carol has a prayer group at her house every Wednesday night where a group of women from her synagogue urge God to help find mates for women who are still single and searching.

Barry and I hadn't been saving money for the marriage of our sons, or to support them for life. Instead we invested in the education and credentials they would need to have the potential to make a living. We never spent even a second discussing Carter or Tyler's weddings. The thought had never even entered our minds. It was a given that our boys, being smart, sensitive, good-looking, fun to be with, and kind human beings would each find a woman one day who they would marry. Barry and I would be responsible for whatever it is that parents of the groom pay for – most likely the rehearsal dinner and the honeymoon. That might cost us $10,000 or so. Before I left for Israel, Barry and I had been informed about the Jewish wedding custom of the groom's parents paying for FLOPS. That acronym stands for flowers, liquor, orchestra, photographers, and sheitel (rhymes with cradle and means 'the bride's wig'). We still didn't know how much FLOPS would cost us, but we assumed it would be something reasonable. Shortly after meeting the Rosenthal's, the dinner discussion turned to the wedding. Carol wanted to know how many people we'd be inviting. She already had the seating chart and vendor names and numbers from Rachel's wedding, so she was ready and raring to hit the ground running. I told Carol that I didn't have a clue as to the number of people we would be having, and we didn't have a problem if Carter and Naomi wanted to elope. I wanted them to know that the wedding event itself was no "biggie" for us. Then Stuart started talking about the band he wanted to hire for the wedding. They had been recommended by the wife of the rabbi at their synagogue, and he asked me to trust him on his choice. I asked him if the band would play popular music and was informed that only Jewish music would be playing the entire time. This would help everyone keep God top-of-mind. I wasn't at all happy about not being able to shimmy to Sheryl Crow's, "All I Wanna Do is Have Some Fun," especially if we had to pay for it. I started thinking that the wedding wouldn't be any fun for me. I took the plunge and asked the Rosenthal's what FLOPS was going to cost us, and they said that our portion would be $20-$25,000. I realized then that this was going to be a Carol and Stuart affair. Naomi is so easy-going and in love that if Carter and her got married under a chuppah on the beach, she couldn't be happier. But her parents' dream was to have the "wedding of the year" as would be appropriate for a co-president of the synagogue. Mind you, this was the same day that I bought the diamond ring for Naomi. It had been exactly a month since Carter and Naomi met, and we were already dropping money like it was going out of style. We had paid a bundle for Carter to attend and graduate from the University of Pennsylvania, had been subsidizing him in Israel, and had hoped that we were off the hook for any other major expenses. In our dreams! I excused myself and called Barry at home and told him I didn't consider myself a very good representative for our family. I wanted to get on the next flight home and run away from these people.

When I got back to the table, Stuart and Carol suggested that we should buy Naomi and Carter an apartment in the Old City of Jerusalem. They had offered Carter and Naomi a generous amount of money to help them buy a place. Say what? Naomi, who had been on holiday in Israel for over six weeks with no end in sight because she was now a Jewish woman in love and getting married, and Carter, who has never been remotely close to financial independence, and all the Hard Core Jewish People felt that because Carter is such a Torah whiz kid and they'll bring wonderful Jewish babies into the world, that the parents of Naomi and Carter should set them up with a place to live. My reaction was, "Rent a place like the rest of us did as newlyweds. Where do you guys get off thinking that it's okay to not work and expect others to buy you a house? I don't think freeloading is a great Jewish tradition and I won't go along with that custom. I'd rather give money to suicide bomb victims in Israel who are alive but can't work due to their physical and/or mental injuries. Let the Hard Core Jewish People buy you a house if they think you're so great." My upbringing and work ethic of a day's pay for a day's work made it very difficult for me to understand this arrogance and sense of entitlement that were coming from Naomi and Carter. I was totally grossed-out and wondered how Carter, after only three-and-a-half years in Israel, didn't find all of this holier-than-thou talk as appalling as I did. One thing I had learned since I started studying about Judaism is the importance of being humble. Moses was the most humble person who ever existed. Even though Moses attained the greatest spiritual heights ever reached by a person, he was not proud of his achievements. He felt that God had given him certain skills and abilities and if someone else had been given these traits, that person would have done more with them. Even I knew that there is no place in Judaism for a swelled head or feelings of self-importance. What happened to my child since I saw him four months ago? I said to Carter, "We all look forward to seeing greatness from the Carter-Naomi pairing, but the world hasn't seen it yet. We're all still waiting. Ditch your ego and keep studying Torah so you can become a rabbi and help connect Jews to their heritage. Just being good Jews doesn't connote greatness to me. You've got to impact vast quantities of people to be great."

Walking to dinner the next night which was Shabbat, Carol said to me, "Isn't this just the best weekend of your life?" I answered, "Well, as a matter of fact, I'm having somewhat of a crisis and was crying a few hours ago while sitting on the curb on a street in Jerusalem." I like Carol so much that I wanted her to know we weren't on the same page. I felt extremely pressured to help subsidize a home for Naomi and Carter, and the thought revolted me. Carol understood where I was coming from and was not at all judgmental. After all, back in 1969 she had wanted to go to Woodstock but her mom wouldn't let her. No wonder we could relate, even though we're very different. I told her that personally, I'd rather go on an African safari than contribute to buying an apartment for the new couple. Carter's transition to an Observant Jew had brought us emotionally closer together because he so appreciated our acceptance of his decision to go Hard Core. But this wedding was creating a huge rift between us. Not realizing that I was a woman on the edge, at dinner Stuart leaned over and quietly said to me, "They'll also need a car, ya know." Forget about my previous coping mechanisms of "Xanax-mode" and "whatever." I progressed to "frontal-lobotomy mode" and "Thorazine-mode" (an anti-psychotic medication) and I still wasn't doing well. I needed to be hypnotized to feel okay about helping to buy a house for people who are capable of working for a living. Give me a break. What was this world coming to?

The plan for Saturday was for the Rosenthal's and Schwartz's to meet at 11:30am at the Cardo. This is one of Jerusalem's most conspicuous Roman-Byzantine sites. It's a wide street that goes from one side of the Old City to the other, bordered on the west by massive walls and on the east by an arcade. We were going to walk together from there to Shabbat lunch at one of Carter's rabbi's houses in the Old City. I was so disgusted with Carter and Naomi's self-aggrandizement that I told Carter before we parted Friday night that I might or might not be there the next day. I said it was too hot and it depended upon whether or not I felt like sweating since taking a cab on the Sabbath was illegal procedure.

I ended up going late to the Cardo on Saturday morning and by the time I arrived, there was no one familiar to me in sight. I realized that I needed a reprieve from Carter's over-inflated opinion of himself, and how fortuitous it was that I missed lunch. The walk to the Cardo from my hotel had been a great workout and when I got back to my room, I got on my computer with my iPod playing in the background and started writing an email to my friends and family. I knew that this was a violation of the Sabbath, but my priority was reaching out for advice rather than following halacha (Torah

71

law). I didn't know what to do regarding the pressure I was getting to pay tons of money for a wedding and setting up house for the new couple. To me it seemed like there was no end in sight from the full-court money press that I was experiencing.

Jared, an incredibly sensitive and empathic friend of Carter's from UPenn, came to visit me that afternoon. He had been with us the night before, witnessed the scene, and felt that I might need some moral support. Jared is living in Israel temporarily while going through an Orthodox conversion from Catholicism to Judaism. I was able to read to him what I had written so he could objectively determine if there was anything I said that I might regret later. Jared approved and after he left, I e-mailed my all-points-bulletin "Report from Jerusalem" so everyone would know what condition my condition was in. The responses started pouring in and I got inspirational pearls of wisdom along with sympathy and compassion from my friends and family in the U.S. I needed to know that I wasn't the only one who was aghast at the Jewish custom of buying a home for young couples who are capable of earning a living, simply because they are good Jews and will produce wonderful Jewish children.

I didn't cross paths with Carter or the Rosenthal's on Saturday, and I felt that was therapeutic. I walked into the concierge lounge at my hotel Saturday evening, got a glass of wine, and went outside to the patio overlooking the Old City. There was an older man sitting there who noticed that I was upset, and asked me to join him at his table. I told him that I had divorced my son that day. Carter had become this egotistical person with a sense of entitlement, and I didn't want to have anything to do with him. He expected us to support him and Naomi, even though they are both capable of working. Here was this yeshiva scholar, aspiring to do Jewish outreach (kiruv pronounced KEE-roov), and he had driven away his greatest fan. It didn't make me feel like Carter had a promising future in bringing Jews closer to their heritage. The older man, named Tzadik, told me that I was having a crisis and I needed to talk to a rabbi at Aish HaTorah. It turned out that Tzadik was a big contributor to Aish, and was able to get the home telephone number of the head rabbi (aka the Rosh Yeshiva). We tried reaching the rabbi but with no luck. Nonetheless, Tzadik made me feel better because he didn't think it was unreasonable to expect Carter and Naomi to earn a living.

On Sunday morning, walking on the streets of Jerusalem, Carter called to tell me that he thought a lot about what I said and felt that I was right. He agreed that it was wrong for him and Naomi to act so pompous and presumptuous, and those are not Jewish values. He admitted that they had been "off" course and he was grateful to me for not just sitting there and being complacent about their behavior. It was a giant mitzvah that I held my ground and had the courage to tell them how I feel. He told me he loved me and always wants me to be a part of his life. What a relief! Carter and I were no longer divorced and I was back on the bus. That was fortuitous, because Sunday evening was the engagement party (called a vort in Hebrew), and I was expected to be there and to pay for it. What's another $1,200 when one is spending money like it's going out-of-style.

A vort is the opposite of a roast. Instead of teasing the guests of honor, they praise them. The room was packed with Carter's yeshiva buddies, rabbis from his and other yeshivas, Naomi's family and friends, and my Israeli first cousins and their families. Highly prestigious rabbis spoke about what a passionate, capable, Torah scholar Carter is and how they can't wait to see the achievements of the Carter/Naomi merger. Naomi will be a devoted wife who will create a wonderful environment for herself, her husband, and her children to thrive in. Carter's fellow yeshiva students did a Hans and Franz Saturday Night Live routine to mock his commitment to working out. They teased him about his "look," walking around with his Torah books, water bottles, and an iPod at all times. We all knew that Carter is a dynamo, but until then I had no idea that he was as highly esteemed as he is.

A Visit to Mea Sharim

At the *vort*, the matchmaker, had informed me that it was customary for the parents of the groom to buy the new couple sterling silver candlesticks. These would be used by them for every Shabbat and holiday and something that would last a lifetime. It sounded like a good investment to me, so I was amenable to the suggestion. Monday afternoon, Carter and Naomi picked me up in a cab at my hotel and we headed for Mea Sharim to see my first cousin and his family and to buy candleholders.

Mea Sharim is a neighborhood made up of only ultra-Orthodox Jews, also referred to as Haredi (HA-reedy, meaning those who tremble before God). They live in a cloistered world, distinctly separate, by choice, from Israeli society. They adhere to religious customs far more prohibitive than mainstream Judaism. Their spiritual devotion extends beyond the technical requirements of Jewish religious law. They believe they are living according to the Torah, while modern, secular Israel is considered corrupted by immorality, materialism, and unbelief. They scrupulously maintain the dress, language and faith of Eastern European Jewish communities lost to the Holocaust. Despite high summer thermometer readings, their year-round dress code for men is black suits and hats every day of the week, with perhaps an additional layer of a long black silken overcoat, or a fur hat, for the Sabbath and other festive occasions. For women, it is ankle-length skirts and long-sleeved blouses, heads covered and legs sheathed in tights. Contact with the outside world through television is banned, though they are allowed to use the Internet under rabbinical supervision. Yiddish is the common tongue of the black-garbed men and soberly clad women who hurry along Mea Sharim's narrow streets. Signs warn outsiders to abide by the quarter's rules of modesty, and the use of cameras is forbidden.

My Jewish lineage was something that gave me tons of brownie points the minute Carter moved to Israel. My mom was the youngest of five sisters. Her oldest sister had made *aliyah* (moved from the U.S. to Israel) in 1971 along with her husband and two of her three sons. While my mom couldn't wait to discard Orthodoxy when she married my dad at the age of 18, Aunt Frances was the only one of the five daughters who held firm to her Torah-true life. Carter felt an instant rapport and love for his relatives who became his Israel family, and was amazed at the illustriousness of his ancestry. My cousin, Rabbi Aaron David, is a highly revered Torah scholar, who, like most haredi men, single-mindedly focuses his life on Torah study. Haredim believe that they have a direct promise from God that Torah study, day in and day out, is what keeps the Jewish people alive. Rather than earning a lot of money, haredim prefer living a minimal material life and focusing on more spiritual and moral values to correct the world and society. Aaron and his wife Leah have ten children, and live in a small two-bedroom apartment in the heart of Mea Sharim. Fortunately, some of the children are married now so it's less crowded than it has been. They are completely content with their lot in life and devoted to belief, faith, and performing as many good deeds (mitzvot) as possible. They are the epitome of what a good Jew should be.

We had a great visit and then headed to a sterling silver store that was nearby. Carter and Naomi selected a beautiful set of candlesticks and a tray to match, costing me $1,300. Whatever, it's only money. The whole time we were in the store, Carter was harassing me to chip in a giant chunk of money, like Carol and Stuart had offered, so he and Naomi could buy an apartment in the Old City of Jerusalem. I told him I didn't think it was a good investment, but he wouldn't take no for an answer. He badgered me continuously until I couldn't take it anymore. As I walked out of the store in tears, I said to Naomi: "You're lucky you haven't seen the merciless side of Carter...yet." Then there I was, alone on the streets of Mea Sharim, without a clue as to how to get back to my hotel. Talk about an adventure. I had no Israeli money in my purse so I couldn't take a cab. I couldn't find an ATM in order to buy more money. Worst of all, my phone card that enabled me to use my cell phone had a balance too low for me to make phone calls. I asked a couple of people for directions out of Mea Sharim, but none of them spoke English. Then miraculously, Barry called me. I could receive incoming calls easily; I just couldn't place any calls. Barry recommended that I walk downhill. That was the clue I needed to get me back to my hotel. What a relief when I saw familiar sights.

On Tuesday morning I met Carter, Naomi, and their real estate agent at what I call a "teardown" apartment in the Old City. I was trying to be a good sport and join in their enthusiasm, but it wasn't easy. Visible signs of neglect and water damage were apparent, and it looked like the "money pit" to me – a place that would constantly require repairs. The Carter I used to know would have never considered such a place acceptable. Fortunately I did have some control over the situation because they needed our money in order to buy a place. I tried to make it clear that they could forget about receiving a windfall from us.

Tuesday night I took Carter, Naomi, Motty, and Bala (BAY-la) Burger out to dinner. At the vort the night before, Bala saw that I was troubled by the financial pressure I was getting, and informed me that I did not have to do anything that I felt uncomfortable doing. Whew, what a relief to hear that. Motty and Carter were deeply involved in a conversation regarding being able to unscrew certain wine bottle tops on Shabbat. I interrupted and facetiously told them that from a secular perspective, it's a good thing that they're focusing on bottle caps rather than the Israel economy or any other topic of major importance. Motty smiled and said: "You Secular Jews can discuss those issues and we Orthodox Jews will deal with the nuances of living a Torah life." Even though bottle caps may seem trivial to me, staying true to Torah law and debating picayune details is an important part of Jewish life.

On Wednesday, Naomi and I went to Yad Vashem, the Holocaust Museum in Jerusalem. Reading the stories and hearing actual survivors tell their story on films was heart-wrenching, but we very much enjoyed spending time together. Naomi is just one of those kind, caring, and non-judgmental people who was put on earth to make this world a better place. She told me that she realized she hadn't seen all of Carter's sides, but she knew that she would love and accept him unconditionally. I felt that Carter could not have found a better person to share his life with than Naomi.

Furthermore, Naomi's parents and sister were great people and even though I didn't agree with their customs, I was glad to know them and have them be part of our extended family.

I finally got back to Miami on Thursday afternoon and had to be put through detox in order to join the ranks of the living and not feel like an anti-Semite. It was so great being home and back with my honey. Now our job would be to work on our guest list and whatever else was necessary to prepare for the wedding. I would do my best to not rain on Carol and Stuart's parade.

The Wedding

Wedding Plans

From the time of the engagement until the wedding, the bride and the groom are supposed to abandon all worldly, purposeless, and meaningless activities and focus on improving their spiritual state. This is not the time for rebel yells or dancing in the street. Rather, their focus is to be on studying Torah, performing *mitzvot* (commandments) in an exemplary manner, occupying oneself in the service of prayer, and repenting – truly repenting, in a manner that not only does the penitent forgive him/herself, but that God truly forgives him/her. The pre and post wedding details are supposed to be handled by others so that the bride and groom are not distracted from their true priorities at this time. Fortunately, the couple is permitted to select and try on the clothes they will wear for the wedding.

We had six weeks to prepare for Carter and Naomi's wedding. Being the parents of the groom, we were informed by those "in-the-know" that our job was to smile and write checks. Unfortunately, that's not one of my specialties when it comes to agreeing to things I perceive as ludicrous. But I tried to give it my college-girl all. At one point, Carter informed me that I was taking the joy out of his wedding by complaining about all the expenses. I felt like Steve Martin in "Father of the Bride" and promised him that I would be a better girl in the future. Barry said, "Honey, we can afford this so don't worry about it." I started thinking about how this wedding would bring about an incredible reunion with family and friends, and that's how I rationalized and made myself feel fine about all the money this extravaganza was going to cost us. One has to throw a major bash in order to get people to come from far and wide to converge. How wonderful that the event is a joyful wedding rather than a depressing funeral. Thank you Carter and Naomi for making this happen.

One situation that had to be overcome was Carter's initial adamancy about not having Raven, Tyler's non-Jewish fiancé, at the wedding. That was totally unacceptable to me. I told Carter that he could either have Raven killed or invite her. Not inviting her was not an option. It wasn't nice and God can't possibly want anyone to treat others that way. If Raven didn't come, I wasn't coming. Slowly but surely, Carter came around. He realized how much his brother loved Raven and he became accepting of her being there. Even *Ba'alei Teshuva* (newly Observant Jews) come around in the long run when they realize something is the right thing to do, as long as it doesn't violate Torah law.

Naomi left Israel and returned home to New York on September 4th, but pined away for Carter. They had only first met one month and one week previously, and being so far away was causing her distress. She is one of the calmest people I've ever met, but the thought of not seeing Carter again until mid-October was unacceptable. She ended up returning to Israel for two weeks before going back to New York again. Before she left, I told her that I knew exactly how she felt. Had it been me, I would grab Barry by the scruff of the neck when I saw him at the airport and throw him down and have my way with him. I said to Naomi, "What will you and Carter do – jump up and down and glow like laser lights?" She said, "Exactly." Their love just radiates whenever they are together.

Our top priority was notifying guests, prior to the invitations being ready, that they should cancel their manicures for October 30th and consider parking themselves in New York. Our boy was getting married. Yikes! I also needed to line up a hotel for all of us to stay at because Hurricane Katrina had obliterated New Orleans and a bunch of conventions had been moved to New York. As a Marriott Platinum member, I am guaranteed a room in any Marriott brand hotel with 48 hours advance notice. Yet here I was, with six weeks advance notice, and the Marriott Long Island already could not accommodate me. We finally lined up the Marriott Courtyard Hotel at JFK, and that turned out to be a great location.

Carter didn't leave Jerusalem until October 16th, and then he flew to New York. He and Naomi needed to get a marriage license, open a checking account, and buy a wedding band. They had only one day to accomplish that before the holiday of Sukkot began and before Carter left for Miami. For the first two days of Sukkot, the Jewish People do not go to work and they observe the same rules and regulations as on the

Sabbath. Carter and Naomi managed to get the marriage license and open a checking account, but ran out of time to buy a ring. The wedding ring, however, was a priority. Jewish law requires three things for a couple to be officially married. This includes the signing of a contract (called a *ketubah*), the man giving the woman a smooth unadorned wedding band that he owns or paid for (representing something of value), and consummation. To save them time and fit it into their schedule, Carol had suggested that Carter and Naomi could go buy some "junky" wedding ring locally on Sunday instead of schlepping into the city. Carol said that among her peers, the custom was for the wedding band not to be anything special and many of the brides never wear it again after the wedding. All the rings look alike, simple gold bands, and later on in life when they have more money, the husband sometimes buys his wife a new more expensive wedding band. Inside I felt that if Carter continues along the path he's on, he isn't likely to have discretionary income even down the road. It's now or never for Naomi. I said, "With all due respect, Carol, even though I'm a Secular Jew, I know for a fact that there is nothing ordinary about Naomi and Carter's marriage. According to Rabbi Kaplan who wrote <u>Made in Heaven</u>, the wedding band is supposed to serve as a symbol that Carter will protect Naomi. I don't think that a chintzy ring is appropriate, whether or not this is your custom." Carol said, "Thank you" because she was happy I felt that Naomi deserved a special wedding band. Damn straight!

Sukkot lasts for eight days and *halachically* speaking, Jews are not supposed to purchase new clothes, have clothes mended, or dry cleaned during this time. Fortunately Carter received special permission from one of his rabbis to buy clothes for his wedding. What a break. He wouldn't have to look like a hobo on the most important day of his life. But it was going to be a real challenge finding time to go shopping with him. He arrived in Miami on Thursday, October 20th, and Friday night and Saturday he was incommunicado during *Shabbat*. On Saturday night, Carter ordered a platinum wedding band online for Naomi. He described the rings to her over the telephone and they made the choice together, with him in Miami and her in New York. They opted for a narrow platinum band that Naomi would wear on the same finger as her platinum setting diamond engagement ring.

Things were getting a bit hairy in Miami because Hurricane Wilma was expected to hit on Monday. On Sunday Carter and I headed for The Falls, a beautiful shopping mall with lots of men's stores. Unfortunately, all of the stores were closed due to the anticipation of the hurricane, but I was calm, cool, and collected. It's not lung cancer, so we can deal with it. I'm also very perseverant, so we found a store that was open where we ended up buying his suit. The problem now was going to be finding someone to alter the suit during the day on Monday. Monday at sundown through Wednesday at sundown were the last two days of Sukkot. The second to the last day is called Shemini Atzeret and the last day is the holiday of Simchat Torah. No work is allowed on those days, and that includes anyone working on altering

Carter's suit for his wedding. That meant that if the suit wasn't altered during the day on Monday, we'd have to wait until Wednesday night. Carter was going back to New York on Thursday, October 27th and we were heading there on October 28th. The wedding was on October 30th.

As expected, Hurricane Wilma hit Miami from around 7a-10a Monday morning. It was only a Category 1, but 74-95 mph winds for three or so hours can do their fair share of damage. No one was working that day, not to mention tailors. Barry and I found some chalk in the house and made marks on Carter's suit as to where tailoring was needed. Since neither of us has had any experience in this arena, I figured that the chances of the suit fitting right after being altered were remote. Oh well. If worst comes to worst, Carter will wear a black suit that isn't brand new. He will be wearing a white *shmatte* (called a *kittel*) over his suit anyway during the wedding. After the wedding, he'll take off the kittel and also remove his jacket for dancing. In my opinion, the suit was optional but the wedding ring was not. I was concerned about the status of the wedding band Carter had ordered online Saturday night, because no mail was being delivered and Fed Ex was not operating. Hurricane Wilma had been such a widespread storm that half of Miami was still without power. The airport was closed and we didn't have electricity or a landline until Wednesday afternoon, but at least we still had water pressure. As Carter's administrative assistant, I took it upon myself to violate the second to the last day of Sukkot on Tuesday and call to find out if we would have the ring before we boarded the plane on

Friday. It's a good thing that I was willing to risk God's wrath and make that call because it turned out that all platinum rings are custom made by this company. Even though their web site said that the turnaround time is three days, for a platinum ring, it would be two weeks. I informed them that we needed the ring in our hot little hands no later than 10:30am on Friday. They understood the urgency of the situation and got the ring shipped out on Wednesday to arrive on Thursday. My girlfriend resolved the suit-alteration situation by lining up a tailor who was willing to accommodate Carter's religious requirements. This person worked on the suit between 8p-10p Wednesday night and miraculously, it fit him perfectly. We were moving right along and not overly-concerned about the impediments caused by the hurricane aftermath. If the airport wasn't open on Thursday, Carter would drive up to New York. If the ring didn't arrive in time, Carter would have to use a temporary replacement until he received the one he ordered. We had options. Wedding invitees were calling us on Wednesday night to see if the event was still on in spite of the hurricane. I told them we would not let some little hurricane come between Carter and Naomi's wedding. As it turned out, on Thursday 50% of the flights were leaving Miami International Airport, and Carter's was one of them. But the ring had still not arrived. When I checked the status of the ring on the FedEx website, it indicated that delivery was guaranteed by 3pm that day. However, Fed Ex was still not up-to-speed in Miami so 3pm came and went with no ring in sight. Barry called Fed Ex at 6pm and pleaded his case, and they completely understood the importance of the wedding ring getting to Miami by the next morning. Unfortunately they still couldn't guarantee the arrival of any packages yet, because their communications systems in Miami weren't up-to-speed. In the end, Fed Ex rose to the occasion and on Friday morning at 9am, Barry picked up the ring. We left for New York with the ring in hand and everything was falling into place.

Pre-Wedding Events

I really had never been to or participated in an Orthodox Jewish wedding, so I thought it might be a nice touch for us to have a rehearsal before the actual event. However, the Rosenthal family was confident that I would do fine and didn't feel a need for us to practice. If they weren't worried, I wasn't at all concerned. I told Carol that she could put a leash on me and I'd follow her lead.

One week before a traditional Jewish wedding, the bride and groom stop seeing and talking to each other in order to enhance the joy of their wedding through their separation. On Saturday morning, the day before the wedding, at Carol and Stuart's synagogue, a special ceremony was arranged for Carter known as an *Aufruf* (pronounced OOF-roof). Since there was no hotel within walking distance of Carol and Stuart's synagogue and since our friends and family would be staying at the same hotel as us, there was no way we were going to park ourselves at a stranger's house in Queens, New York for 25 hours so we could walk to the Aufruf. Carter preferred for us not to attend the event than violate the Sabbath by driving, and besides he felt that it was no big deal if we weren't at the Aufruf. The event involved him going to the synagogue and taking an active part in the service, as well as announcing the impending wedding to the congregation. Then the congregation threw bags of candies at him, with younger members of the community tending to throw harder but in a jovial manner. We missed the Aufruf for a good reason, and Carol said that all of her friends understood the appropriateness of us being at the hotel with family and friends who had flown to New York to be with us. Barry and I had dear friends who came up from Miami, Tyler and Raven flew in, my brother and sister-in-law were there from Colorado, and friends and family from neighboring states and New York were all there. My stepmother who I hadn't seen in 14 years came in for the occasion, as did my 92-year old aunt from Las Vegas – my mom's only remaining sister.

On Saturday night, we threw an intimate dinner for about 40 friends and family members at a *kosher* Chinese restaurant on Long Island. It was such a great way for us to get together and have time to truly schmooze before the 375-person wedding the next night. My first cousins, Aaron and Avishai David from Israel attended, as well as other more distant cousins I had never met before. [Avishai is the rosh yeshiva (boss man) of a post-high school yeshiva close to Jerusalem.] We flew in the matchmaker from Israel and the rabbi and *rebbetzin* (rabbi's wife) from Young Israel in Miami. It was a heart-warming reunion that was priceless.

Aaron had not left Israel for thirty-five years, and relatives who hadn't seen him for ages were so surprised that he was there. They were moved that Aaron thought so highly of Carter that he was willing to leave the security of Mea Sharim *(See Section I, "Checking Out the Scene in Israel" Chapter)* and subject himself to the evils of New York. Carter met Raven in person for the first time that night, and he was sincerely happy to see her. Raven and I couldn't stop marveling about that afterwards, because of the long journey it took for her to gain Carter's acceptance. Jewish People, in an effort to deter mixed marriages, do not condone or accept mixed marriages so Carter has never been supportive of Tyler being with Raven. Carter probably won't attend Tyler and Raven's wedding because of that, even though he dearly loves his brother. He should, however, attend the celebration but we'll see what happens when the time comes. It's all about flexibility. It definitely would not be a Torah violation.

The Happening Itself

You had to be at the wedding in order to comprehend the scene there with Observant Jews, Secular Jews, and non-Jews all merging together for a very special occasion. This included Carter's fraternity brothers from UPenn and friends he grew up with in Miami. The scenario for a traditional Jewish wedding goes as follows:

- Prior to the main ceremony, the wedding begins with the groom's signing of the *ketubah*, the Jewish marriage contract, which sets out the legal terms of the marriage. The ketubah, written in Aramaic, details the husband's obligations to provide his wife with food, clothing, shelter, and sexual relations. The signing is done in the presence of at least two Orthodox Jewish witnesses.

- Separate receptions are held for the bride and groom to hold court and be honored by their guests. The bride sits like a queen on a throne, receiving greetings and blessings from all of the female wedding guests who are treated to profuse quantities of refreshments and hors d/oeuvres. Male guests go to a groom's table where, after the signing of the ketubah, the groom is treated like a king and everyone chants, sings, and tells jokes. Light snacks are served along with hard liquor for the traditional *lechaims* (the Jewish salute when drinking, which means, "to life!")

- When the bride is ready, she sends a delegation to the groom's table to invite the men to the *bedeken* (veiling), which is the last ceremony before the wedding begins. The groom, together with his father and future father-in-law, is accompanied by musicians and male guests to the room where the bride is receiving her guests. The groom, who has not seen nor spoken to his bride for a week (an eternity for a young couple in love), does the veiling in which he places the veil over the bride's face. One of the reasons given for the ceremony is related to modesty; the veil symbolically represents the added level of modesty the bride is expected to adopt with her elevation to the married state. Another explanation is that the veiling underscores, from this day on, that the beauty of the bride is reserved for her husband alone to appreciate. Others view the ritual as a symbolic act that emphasizes the importance of the bride's soul and character over her physical attractiveness.

The Ceremony

- The men sit on the right side of the chapel and the women on the left. The ceremony itself lasts approximately 45 minutes. A Jewish wedding is, above all, a family affair. There is no firm rule about who escorts the bride to the *chuppah* (wedding canopy). Jewish law does not govern the makeup of the procession, and so couples are free to decide the exact arrangement of their procession. Sometimes grandparents follow the rabbi, followed by the ushers, the Best Man, the groom and his parents, the bridesmaids, the Maid of Honor, and finally the bride and her parents. Candles may be carried by escorts and attendants symbolizing the oneness that will come about as the couple is united under the chuppah. Live Jewish music during the procession is an old tradition that sets the mood and the pace of the occasion. Barry and I walked Carter down the aisle and Carol and Stuart walked with Naomi. I wore a gold lace veil over my hair to show respect for the sacredness of the occasion. After the ceremony, I used the veil to tie my hair in a ponytail.

- Once we were under the chuppah, Barry and I put a white bathrobe-type garment on Carter over his clothes, called a *kittel*. After the wedding ceremony, Carter removed the garment which is intended to be a reminder to Carter of the white shrouds that he will wear when he dies.

- The arrangement of the wedding party under the chuppah is not specified in Jewish law. Upon reaching the chuppah, the bride circles the groom seven times. Carol and I held Naomi's train and walked around Carter with her. Circling the groom is a very old custom, the meaning and origin of which has no consensus. According to aish.com, "just as the world was created in seven days, the bride is figuratively building the walls of the couple's new home. The number seven also symbolizes the wholeness and completeness that they cannot attain separately."

- The Jewish wedding ceremony involves two phases. The first part is the *kiddushin*, which is actually the betrothal ceremony bonding two souls into one with each other and with God. The rabbi greets everyone and makes two blessings over a cup of wine. The bride and groom drink their first sips from one of the two cups of wine used during the ceremony.

- Next comes the ring, which is the essential part of the ceremony. The Best Man, Tyler in this case, hands the groom the ring and he places it on the index finger of the bride's right hand, the finger thought to be directly connected to the heart. The groom repeats the blessing, "Behold you are consecrated to me with this ring according to the laws of Moses and Israel." Traditionally, there is no verbal response on the part of the bride. By accepting the ring, it signifies her approval. This is officially the act of kiddushin, the betrothal of the couple. Jewish law now considers them married and the first phase of the ceremony is completed.

- Regarding the ring, it must personally belong to the groom and cannot be borrowed. It must be a complete circle without a break to emphasize the hope for a harmonious marriage. Finally, the ring must be plain without stones or decoration. The plainness and simplicity of the ring are held by some to represent the wisdom that a good marriage is attainable by all, rich and poor alike. The ring's value must be known to the wife so that there can be no claim that the husband deceived her into marrying by misleading her as to its value. Orthodox rabbis generally do not permit a double ring ceremony because the protocol of a Jewish wedding ceremony has a number of integral elements to it that may not be interrupted by the introduction of additional elements.

- The text of the ketubah is read aloud in Aramaic, often repeated in English. The ketubah is then stored away for safe keeping or it may be displayed on an easel for guests to inspect. The officiator [in this case it was my first cousin Avishai David from Israel] will then make a speech about the couple and bless them as they begin their new life together.

- Next comes the second part of the wedding ceremony, which is referred to as the *nisuin*, the nuptials or spiritual elevation. The bride and groom remain beneath the chuppah. Seven nuptial blessing are recited by seven different people. They are called up separately to the chuppah and are honored with a blessing, a *bracha*, to recite in front of the *chassan* (groom) and *kallah* (bride). These blessings acknowledge the creation of humanity not only in a physical sense but in a spiritual sense, transcending time and spanning the generations of Jewish existence. While only the last two blessings mention the chassan and kallah explicitly, read as a whole the seven blessings place the couple in the chain of Jewish history and express their wish for personal and universal joy and peace. The newlyweds then drink from the second cup of wine.

- The ceremony ends with the groom's smashing of a glass or a small symbolic piece of glass with his right foot. It symbolizes the destruction of the second Holy *Temple* in Jerusalem, the frailty of human relationships, and the existence of human suffering. This action is a personal reminder that just as we accept joy into our lives, we recognize that there may also be times of sorrow.

After the Ceremony

- Immediately after the ceremony, before receiving congratulations from their guests, the couple retires to a *yichud* room (pronounced YICK-hod) where they spend ten or fifteen minutes together alone in seclusion. They are escorted to the room by witnesses and the door is closed. Here they can touch for the very first time. The emotions of the moment have got to be almost overwhelming. We all wish we could mainline that feeling on a daily basis.

- The chassan and kallah then rejoin their guests amid great joy, singing, and dancing. The Jewish wedding is unique in that there is an explicit *mitzvah* (commandment) to help the bride and groom rejoice. The active celebration of each guest enhances the personal joy of both the bride and the groom. The blessing is said over the *challah* (bread) and a festive meal is served. Upon completion of the meal, grace is recited with a repetition of the *sheva brachot*, the seven blessings that were recited under the chuppah. Exuberant Jewish music and dancing traditionally accompany the ceremony and the reception. However, even while rejoicing, the Jewish People are not supposed to forget their reverence and awe of God.

- Instead of leaving on a honeymoon, Jewish custom dictates that the couple begins their new life together in their community. For seven consecutive evenings following the wedding, it is customary that friends or relatives host festive meals in their honor. The act of feasting recalls the "seven-day celebration" after the marriage of Jacob to Leah, while spending their days in prayer, learning Torah and performing mitzvot in order to give their "new house in Israel" a solid foundation in God's ways of holiness.

My Take on the Wedding

The wedding was beautiful and everyone had a wonderful time. But I had a problem with the bombardment of photographers/paparazzi that seemed incongruous with what one would expect during the central moment of the traditional Jewish wedding ceremony when the couple is considered officially married. At the time when Carter and Naomi were under the chuppah and Carter put the ring on Naomi's finger and said: "Behold, you are betrothed unto me with this ring according to the laws of Moses and Israel," none of our guests could see a thing. There were ten photographers with bright lights forming a blockade in front of the chuppah obliterating the view for everyone. I felt like a French fry with all the lights baking me to a crisp. In Rabbi Kaplan's book <u>Made in Heaven,</u> he makes it very clear that photographers are allowed at weddings but they must be unobtrusive. "As long as the photographer remains unobtrusive, his presence will not in any way detract from the sanctity and spirit of the occasion." The photographers at this wedding were anything but unobtrusive and during the blessings of betrothal, they obliterated the holiness of the moment.   But that's the custom among many New York Orthodox Jews – the pictures take priority over halacha.

Men and women dance separately at Orthodox Jewish weddings. As a matter of fact, Carter will never dance in public with a woman again including Naomi. He can boogie like crazy with her in the privacy of their home but not out in public. That's just the way things are done. A bummer for me was that the only dance the girls did was a circle dance that has no name. It's a variation-on-a-theme of the hora. Over and over again, everyone has to dance in a circle doing the same steps – no pairing off allowed except for Naomi when she grabbed one of us to dance with her. I wanted to do some other dances but no dice. Grin and bear it. The men, on the other hand, were allowed to do a variety of dances and many of them performed for Carter to entertain him. It was enjoyable watching them.

On Monday, the day after the wedding, we attended the first of seven dinners for Carter and Naomi. The meal was held at Carol and Stuart's rabbi's house. I was talking to a former teacher of Naomi's who is a member of the Rosenthal's synagogue and has always been impressed with Naomi because of her search for Torah truth. She was telling me about her son's Bar Mitzvah and first asked, "Do you know what a Bar Mitzvah is?" I called across the room: "Hey Barry, she wants to know if I know what a Bar Mitzvah is." I then told Naomi's former teacher that my gardener knows what a Bar Mitzvah is. I thought it was hysterical that her perception was such that if someone is not an Observant Jew, then he/she has no knowledge of Judaism. What a mind-boggler. Others attending the dinner also gave me the impression that they view Barry and me as goys (non Jews) because we don't keep kosher and we don't observe Shabbat. I feel like I know more about Judaism than some Orthodox Jews who are caught up in the rules and rituals rather than having a clue as to how to treat others. Where do we go from here?

All in all, I enjoyed the wedding but I'd rather not go to anymore Orthodox Jewish weddings, if possible. I wanted to make pins for guests to wear that had "Hugger" or "Hugger with a diagonal line through it" so I would know who of the opposite sex was okay to hug or shake hands with. The Jewish music doesn't have the beat that makes me want to move my feet, and even if it did, I would be limited to only dancing the circle dance that I don't really care for. While I am very respectful of Orthodox Jews when I am in their presence, I prefer being able to let my hair down and not worry about violating any of the multitudes of rules, regulations, and/or customs associated even with their social occasions. Orthodox Judaism is just too restrictive for me, but I wouldn't have missed Carter and Naomi's wedding for anything.

SECTION II: WHAT'S JUDAISM ALL ABOUT?

Who Are These Ba'al Teshuva (BT) People?

By their nature, BTs (newly Observant Jews) are idealists. They didn't become Orthodox because they were afraid or because they needed a militaristic set of commands for living their lives. They chose Orthodoxy because it satisfied their need for intellectual stimulation and emotional security. Everything one needs to know about how to live properly is in the *Torah*. The very definition of the word "Torah" is God's Instructions for Living. By doing what God wants them to do, BTs feel a sense of freedom from anxiety and worry because they rely and trust in God to look out for their best interests. Waking up in the morning and knowing exactly what God expects of them gives BTs peace of mind. They find the regimentation and predictability of Orthodox Judaism to be a very appealing way of life. As the BT increases his/her knowledge and the feeling of closeness to God, the pleasure received from this accomplishment is very reinforcing and he/she gets into it more and more. For someone who is *frum* from birth (pronounced froom and also referred to as FFB or born and raised as an Orthodox Jew), they are very comfortable with the life they live and do not question the strict and rigid rules because this is the status quo. They didn't choose this life – they inherited it. But for someone who has been on the dark side, becoming observant is a huge deal because they do know what they're missing and yet still choose to fight temptation and live a Jewish life. For them, the pleasure they get by following Torah law is worth the sacrifices they have to make.

The ba'al teshuva movement – the return to traditional Judaism by a number of young Jews who had heretofore been estranged from it, has brought a renewed passion and energy to traditional Jewish life and community, even to those Jews who were born and raised as Orthodox Jews. From *Abraham* onward, there has been an unbroken chain of Jewish tradition passed along from father to son, teacher to student. This chain has enabled the *Jewish Nation* to defy famine, conquest, dispersion, expulsion, and oppression that would have resigned them to the dusty historical tomes of other nations. Carter's pursuit of his heritage gave him the courage to defy the mores and culture of our society and even the family that reared him in order to not let our family's Jewish chain break with his generation.

Yeshiva-Slug Mentality

Truth be told, not all newly Observant Jews who park themselves in a yeshiva all day to study Torah have the potential to be rabbis or great religious leaders and authorities. Learning Torah requires a high level of scholarship and intellect, and not everyone has those qualities. Yet large segments of Orthodox society place a premium on learning Torah full-time, to the extent that working to earn a living, familiarizing and involving oneself with worldly concerns, and even taking time to maintain a physically healthy lifestyle are not encouraged. There are some BTs who are yeshiva slugs that are learning Torah for the sake of learning or for the purpose of self-aggrandizement. Further, some of the BTs have no or minimal secular college education and aren't qualified to do anything else in the labor market. Warehousing themselves in a yeshiva keeps them from having to think about what they want to do in life, and eliminates fear of failure feelings. They don't mind being poverty-stricken or living off of charity. They're performing a mitzvah that God commanded them to do so they feel self-righteous. This is not considered acceptable in Judaism. Torah study is not supposed to be an end unto itself. Learning for the sake of learning implies that learning Torah is an aimless, self-contained pursuit. In fact, Judaism emphasizes that learning Torah is of supreme importance precisely because it leads to or should lead to positive action. This is the highest expression of Torah itself, whether that action takes the form of a professional occupation or of extending oneself to benefit the community.

Orthodox Judaism: A Guide for the Perplexed

They Know We Think They're Weird

First and foremost, you have to understand that the Jewish People realize that they look and act differently than the rest of us. God commanded them not to blend in and assimilate into the population, and they took that commandment seriously like they do most things. They don't care if we think they're weirdos. They are trying to be as close to God as possible by centering their lives on fulfilling commandments in the *Torah*. Traditional Judaism is a comprehensive way of life, filled with rules and practices that affect every aspect of life: what you do when you wake up in the morning, what you can and cannot eat, what you can and cannot wear, how to groom yourself, how to conduct business, who you can marry, how to observe the holidays and *Shabbat*, and perhaps most importantly, how to treat God, other people, and animals. Hard Core Jewish People believe that adhering to Jewish law brings them to a heightened sensitivity between themselves and God. In today's topsy-turvy world, they like knowing how God expects them to be. Judaism is their religion and their way of life.

Not all people who call themselves Orthodox Jews are living the way God intended them to. A good example of this is Jack Abramoff, the super-lobbyist in Washington, DC who was busted in January 2006 for fraud, tax evasion, and conspiracy to bribe public officials. He considers himself an Orthodox Jew and even used some of his secret kickback money to help finance a religious academy in Maryland where he sends his children as well as a sniper school for Israelis on the West Bank. Abramoff and other pseudo-Orthodox Jews' are not living up to the high ideals of Torah, and their behavior should not be considered as representative of all Orthodox Jews. Some of the pseudo-Orthodox Jews pray when they're supposed to, observe the laws of the *Sabbath*, the men wear a kippa (yarmulke), married women wear a wig, they keep kosher, and they observe the laws of Family Purity *(See Section II, "Hard Core Jewish Women: Laws of Family Purity" Chapter)*. But they think it's okay to butt in front of others in line or break the law or they feel superior because they believe they're such good Jews. What about the black hat guy who I came upon in the Old City of Jerusalem and asked directions? He didn't even acknowledge my existence in this universe. Intuitively one would think that God does not want His children to be cold and unfeeling creatures. Yet some of them are. What about the pseudo-Orthodox Jews at Carter and Naomi's wedding who pushed their way to the front of the hors d'oerves lines, or the people who took piles of pastries for the road leaving none for guests who left after them? Being a good Jew and a moral person is a constant struggle, even for the Hard Core Jewish People. All mortals have the ability to fall prey to the evil impulses of pride, greed, envy, hate. If this potential is not checked, people can easily abuse the rights of others.

Jewish laws are therefore needed to remind personkind that everyone will benefit if the rights of all are protected.

So What Does Orthodox Judaism Really Involve?

It is important to recognize that Orthodox Judaism is very diverse, and includes an entire spectrum of beliefs, customs, and modes of behavior. Certainly not everyone who considers themselves an Orthodox Jew follows all of the 613 Torah obligations. Who can blame them, considering the inanity of some of the requirements?

There are some Torah laws and Jewish practices that I really like including:

- Judaism places great stress on proper treatment of animals. Unnecessary cruelty to animals is strictly forbidden, and in many cases, animals are accorded the same sensitivity as human beings.

- Judaism values sex and encourages the enjoyment and pleasuring of the partners in a relationship. A man who consistently refuses to engage in sexual relations with his wife is obligated to grant her a divorce.

- Regarding foreplay, one passage in the Talmud states, "a man may do whatever he pleases with his wife." In fact, there are passages in the Talmud that encourage foreplay to arouse the woman. *Maimonides* (a 12th century Torah scholar who Carter thinks highly of) asserted that a husband "may kiss any organ he wishes. And he may have intercourse in a natural or unnatural manner as long as he does not expend semen to no purpose".

- *Tikkun Olam*, a central precept of Judaism, is repair of the world through the pursuit of social justice. According to the Statement of Principles of Adat Shalom, the mitzvah of *tikkun olam* obliges Jews to help alleviate hunger, homelessness, disease, ignorance, abuse, and political oppression among all people. In addition, Jews have a responsibility to preserve the health of the global ecosystem upon which all life depends. If everyone pursued this mission, what a great world it would be.

Then there are some Torah laws and Jewish practices that really turn me off including:

- Observant Jews have an obstinacy and unwavering adherence to their faith. They are so afraid of diluting traditional Judaism that they refuse to deviate in any way from the written and oral Torah, regardless of the repercussions. I read a story about a woman whose husband was dying and she couldn't touch him because she had her period and was considered *niddah*. She said that keeping true to the Torah was more important than holding her husband's hand before he died. [Haven't these people ever heard of Torah-truish?]

- In Judaism, pride is considered a bad trait and its opposite, humility, is a good one. Remember the SNL Wayne and Garth (Mike Myers/Dana Carvey) routine in which Dana Carvey says, "I'm not worthy. I'm not worthy." Well Torah-true Jews feel like they're nothing compared to God. They believe that all of their talents, wisdom, intelligence — everything they possess — are gifts from *Hashem* to help them fulfill their purpose in life. Thus any glory and honor belongs solely to Hashem, Who equipped them with everything they need to carry out their mission. All their achievements in life should focus only on bringing glory and honor to Hashem and sanctifying His Name. They feel undeserving of receiving credit for any good things they accomplish.

- Because of that damn *Covenant*, Jews have the obligation of repairing the world through social action. That's a heavy burden to accept. They also get the blame for all that is wrong with the world. It seems like they're always praying, mourning, or fasting to repent for all of the sins of the rest of the world.

- *Shomer Negiah* (SHOW-mare nuh-GIE-uh, "to guard the touch to avoid carnal sins") is the practice of avoiding any physical contact with members of the opposite sex, except one's spouse, parent, grandparent, sibling(s), or in medical emergencies. Orthodox men will not even shake hands with a woman and vice versa. You know how fanatical they can be. The main purpose of shomer negiah is to restrict physical contact between unmarried men and women as a safeguard against the development of improper relationships and pre-marital intimacy. Not surprisingly, the Jewish People have taken this commandment too far. Acquaintances may put their hand out to shake with someone and the Observant Jew rejects the handshake. How warm and loving do you think that makes non-Orthodox Jews feel? I warned all of Carter's wedding guests in advance not to violate shomer negiah. With advance notice, we still think that it's a ludicrous requirement but at least we know not to hug or touch so we don't embarrass ourselves. Carter had to get permission from a rabbi for Naomi's 92-year old grandmother, an Auschwitz survivor, to touch him or hug him. As long as she was the initiator, it was legal procedure. [Whatever!]

• Only a man can institute a divorce in Judaism. Unless a woman gets permission from her husband to divorce him—called a "get"—she cannot officially divorce him. Some husbands withhold them out of vindictiveness or to extort financial or custody settlements from their wives. Women denied gets are forbidden from remarrying or even dating, and are called "agunot" or "chained women."

An Overview of Orthodox Jewish Beliefs and Rituals

Men and Women Separated
Men and women must be separated during prayer, usually by a wall or curtain called a *mechitzah* or by placing women in a

second floor balcony. There are two reasons for this: first, your mind is supposed to be on prayer, not on the pretty girl praying near you. Second, many pagan religious ceremonies at the time Judaism was founded involved sexual activity and orgies, and the separation prevents or at least discourages this. [Thank goodness for the mechitzah. An orgy in the synagogue would certainly not be cool.] The bottom line for the practice of separating men and women is that the Torah sages and scholars over the years think of men as horny hooligans who need to be controlled. They cannot be trusted to control themselves.

Same Sex Dancing
Men and women dance separately at weddings and Bar Mitzvahs. In fact men and women never dance together in public – not even husbands and wives. It's all part of the modesty ritual of keeping everything private. *(See Section II, "Hard Core Jewish Women" Chapter)*

Masturbation
Jewish law clearly prohibits male masturbation. The issue is somewhat less clear for women. Obviously, spilling the seed is not going to happen in female masturbation, and there is no explicit Torah prohibition against female masturbation. Nevertheless, Judaism generally frowns upon female masturbation as "impure thoughts" and way too pleasurable.

Homosexuality
Being sexually attracted to people of the same sex or having a homosexual orientation does not violate *halacha* (Jewish

law) in any way. Halacha only addresses behavior and conduct; it does not attempt to control feelings or sexual attractions. However, Jewish law forbids homosexual acts and considers them sinful. This dates back to the Biblical book of Leviticus, which describes sexual intercourse between males as an "abomination" that may be subject to capital punishment (in Biblical times).

Birth Control
Birth control pills are permitted by Torah law but you must first get approval from a rabbi. According to halacha, ejaculation of semen should take place only in the context of vaginal intercourse. No wasting of seed is allowed such as withdrawal from the vaginal before ejaculation or oral ejaculation. Barrier methods of contraception that do not allow the flow of semen into the vagina are prohibited such as IUDs, sponges, and diaphragms.

Don't Say "Mazel Tov" to a Pregnant Woman
The traditional Jewish saying upon hearing of a pregnancy or greeting a pregnant woman is not "*mazel tov*" but "*be'sha'ah tovah*" — may it be at the right time. This avoids tempting fate with premature congratulations. The Jewish People are not into counting their chickens before they're hatched. For the first child, not a single baby item is purchased in advance, which obviously rules out baby showers.

Prayers While Pregnant
The rabbis of the Talmud (Oral law) instructed expecting women and their husbands to pray during the first forty days

of pregnancy about the gender of the baby, male or female (if they had a preference), from forty days to three months for a healthy and whole baby, from three months to six months that the child they have will live, and from six months to nine months for a safe birth.

Abortion
Jewish law allows abortion only if it is necessary to save the mother's life prior to birth. Sometimes it is permitted within the first 40 days of pregnancy and in other special circumstances, but a rabbi must always be consulted first.

When the Wife is in Labor
Observant Jewish husbands, while extremely supportive and helpful through the labor and delivery process, will not touch their wives or hand them things directly during active labor because the women are considered "ritually impure." Furthermore, she still has cooties for several days following delivery when he cannot touch her. There are a different number of days of abstention for male and female babies. *(See Section II, "Hard Core Jewish Women: Laws of Family Purity" Chapter)*

Bris - Jewish Ritual Circumcision
Jewish baby boys must undergo religious circumcision, called a *bris*, on the eighth day of life, even if the eighth day occurs on Shabbat or a holiday. Medical circumcision is prohibited. Judaism views *circumcision* as a religious ceremony, rather than just as surgery.

When a child is circumcised, he is accepted into the "Covenant of *Abraham.*" A Jew who is not properly circumcised is not considered a full Jew. The circumcision must be performed by a qualified mohel or is considered invalid. A mohel is a Jew who has been trained in the physical procedures of circumcision and understands the religious significance of the ritual. At the ceremony, the baby is also given his Hebrew name.

Oral Blood-Sucking Controversy

[Xanax-mode alert!] Following a circumcision, the *Talmud* states that "covenantal blood" must flow from the wound lest a dangerous situation arise. Sucking the blood out through the mouth *(metzitzah b'peh)* was the most efficient way that rabbis could think of to accomplish this in the olden days. That was before we knew anything about bacteria or viruses. Subsequently due to health concerns, many great Orthodox Jewish leaders in the 19th and 20th centuries held that direct oral contact in *metzitzah b'peh* was not a requirement of Jewish law, and that it was halachically acceptable to draw the blood by using a glass pipe or other vacuum-producing implement. Yet the ultra-Orthodox felt then and still feel now that the elimination of oral suction would pose a risk to the child because the blood can't be extracted from the "furthest reaches" when using a glass tube. In 2004, three babies in New York City were found to be infected with herpes after undergoing the oral ritual by a Monsey, NJ based rabbi. All became very sick, one died, and one suffered brain damage. The mohel agreed to stop sucking infant's penises (what a guy) but after the New York City

Health Department had two more cases reported in 2005, they formally recommended that infants not undergo oral-suction circumcisions. The ultra-Orthodox still persist because they do not believe that the evidence is factual and they are very committed to not modifying customs and traditions that they do not feel are potentially harmful. They also believe that no harm will befall those involved in a mitzvah. [Whatever!]

Purpose of Circumcision

In his The Guide of the Perplexed, *Maimonides* asserts that "the bodily pain caused to that member [the penis] is the real purpose of circumcision." His take on the ritual is that it's primarily for the purpose of suppressing the animal urges of men. "For if at birth this member has been made to bleed and has had its covering taken away from it, it must indubitably be weakened."

The Term "Orthodox"

Many Observant Jews do not like or accept the label "Orthodox" because the term never existed until the mid 19th century. Until 1840, 90% of the Jewish world was in Europe and there was only one kind of Judaism.

Orthodox Judaism Has More Than One Version

Unlike Reform and Conservative Judaism, Orthodoxy is not a unified movement with a single governing body. While all Orthodox movements are similar in their beliefs and observance, they differ in the details that are emphasized in their attitudes toward modern culture and the State of Israel.

Modern Orthodox tends to be a bit more liberal and more Zionistic. Ultra-Orthodoxy, including *Yeshivah* movements and the *Hassidic* sect, tend to be the least open to change and the most critical of modern society.

There Are Two Torahs

There are actually two Torahs in Judaism: a Written Torah and an Oral Torah. The Written Torah, also known as the *Tanakh* (pronounced ta-KNOCH – you're supposed to do that gargling sound at the end), does not provide instructions or specifics on how to fulfill the different commandments. Instead, the Oral Torah or *Talmud*, is what Hard Cores rely upon for the interpretation and application of Torah laws. Jewish sages and great Torah scholars are in charge of passing on the Oral Torah from generation to generation. According to tradition, at the time God gave Moses the Torah on Mount Sinai, God also transmitted an Oral Torah which was passed down by word-of-mouth for many, many generations. Finally, after the Destruction of the Second Temple (70 C.E.), when the *Jewish Nation* was threatened with extinction, it became necessary to write down the Oral Torah in order to preserve it.

Routines Facilitate the Performance of Mitzvot

The human body loves patterns (aish.com). Even the most daunting tasks become fluid when set into a schedule. That is why the Torah gives specific times when a mitzvah must be performed. When waking up, for example, Observant Jews say: "Thank God I'm alive." It's a moment of conscious appreciation for getting another chance, another day. If prayer and performing mitzvah become routines, there is less of a chance of forgetting to do them.

Origin of Universe and Life
Ultra-Orthodox Jews, including the Aish HaTorah yeshiva that Carter attends, hold to the book of Genesis literally, that God created the universe/life from nothing, in less than 7 days, less than 10,000 years ago. Adam and Eve were the first humans. However, some hold that a "day" in the Bible is not defined as 24 hours, and some believe that scientific discoveries don't contradict but attest to God's awesome power.

Aish HaTorah has removed some literature from their website that they feel is heretical because it implies that the earth is much older than a literal reading of Genesis would suggest. Rabbi Nosson Slifkin, an ultra-Orthodox author, has had his books blacklisted from the Aish HaTorah website because he asserts that "the Sages were mistaken in certain scientific matters" and "that the world is millions of years old." Another author removed from the aish.com website is nuclear physicist Dr. Gerald Schroeder from the Massachusetts Institute of Technology. Dr. Schroeder, who has resided in Israel for the past twenty years and teaches at the Aish HaTorah Discovery Program in Jerusalem, wrote an essay entitled "The Age of the Universe." Dr. Schroeder "argues that Albert Einstein's Theory of Relativity can be used to reconcile seeming contradictions between the Bible and conventional scientific theories regarding the age of the universe." (Forward Magazine, "Orthodox Rabbis Launch Book Ban" by Steven I. Weiss, 1/21/2005) When informed of aish's website notice, "This article is currently under review, in consultation with today's leading Torah scholars," Dr. Schroeder responded with, "Why would a Torah scholar know relativity, unless he's studied relativity?" [Good point!]

After Death
Traditional Judaism believes in the World To Come, the coming of the messianic age heralded by the *Messiah*, and a resurrection of the dead, but beliefs vary on the details. Some believe souls of the righteous go to heaven, or are reincarnated, while the wicked suffer from a hell of their own making or remain dead. Some believe God will resurrect the righteous to live on earth after the Messiah comes to purify the world. Judaism generally focuses on strictly following God's commandments rather than on details of afterlife or rewards after death.

Why is There Evil in the World?
Most Observant Jews believe God created Satan as an evil inclination, a tendency that lies within everyone. People also have awareness of and an inclination toward goodness. Thus, God provides free will as a test of obedience and faith. If there was no evil in the world, then choosing good would not be an act of free will because one would not have an alternative.

Salvation and Redemption
Salvation is achieved through faith and continual prayer to God, strict adherence to divine commandments (Jewish law), including dietary restrictions, to give to the poor, "love your neighbor as yourself," and to bring God's message to humanity by example (a responsibility of God's "chosen people"). Confessions and repentances are expressed through Yom Kippur when one fasts, asks forgiveness from others and from themselves, and commits to do good deeds in the future. *(See Section II, "Jewish Rituals and Holidays" Chapter)*

Undeserved Suffering
Sometimes it is believed that suffering is caused by a weakness in one's devotion to God. Generally, it is believed that God gave humans free will to feel pleasure and pain, and His purpose in allowing deep suffering of the innocent must be good even if mysterious. God suffers along with the sufferer. Some Jews (e.g. the Hassidim) believe that suffering is punishment for past-life sins. Knowing why God allows suffering is not as important as knowing that God will punish the perpetrators. *(See Section II, "The 'Hurt Me, Hurt Me' Mentality" Chapter)*

Courtesy
Observant Jewish men are not supposed to hold doors open for women because they're not allowed to ogle women's backsides. I said to Carter, "Can't men hold the door open and look the other way?" He said they could but the custom is to not perform that gesture. In Japan, the women hold the

doors open for men so at least Israel hasn't gotten to that point.

Don't Spit

On Shabbat, Observant Jews may not spit on the grass because it could conceivably be considered watering the lawn and that is not allowed. Instead they are instructed that if they have to spit, to do it on the pavement or sidewalk. Very attractive, I'm sure. However, it should be mentioned that according to Torah, one is not supposed to do anything that grosses someone else out. Thus spitting is only acceptable if one is alone or with someone for whom spitting is not offensive.

Fear of Punishment

Hard Core Jewish People adhere to Torah law so they will not be considered sinners, and so that God will not use His power against them. The types of punishment imposed for violating Torah law correspond to the level of violation of God's will. For example, someone who lights a match on the Sabbath will be stoned to death while someone who steals only has to repay what he has stolen. A Jew who intentionally violates the Sabbath is considered as being in denial that God created the universe, and consequently his life is not worth living. Stealing, on the other hand, is more a violation of society than of God's will and so the punishment is more lenient. In reality, the chance of being punished in a Jewish court is remote. Judaism does not actually impose any penalties unless there are two independent, non-related eyewitnesses, who have warned the perpetrator before doing the act as to what punishment he will receive, and the perpetrator must answer them to acknowledge he/she heard.

Only Orthodox Conversions Accepted

Orthodox rabbis do not recognize Jewish conversions performed by non-Orthodox rabbis. This is because non-Orthodox Jews do not require rigid adherence to Jewish law and they might not be as fanatical as they need to be.

No Pierced Ears

No body piercings or violation of the body is allowed including tattoos. Carter had his ear pierced when he was in Middle School, but he didn't know then that it was illegal according to Torah law. He has since repented for that sin and has been forgiven.

No Euthanasia

Life is considered so valuable that the Jewish People are not permitted to do anything that may hasten death, not even to prevent suffering. However, where death is imminent and certain and the patient is suffering, Jewish law does permit one to cease artificially prolonging life.

Women Can't Sing to Men (Kol Isha)

A woman's voice is considering alluring and could cause a man to be aroused or distracted from his prayers. Accordingly, there is a prohibition that women are not supposed to sing when men are present. If a wife is at home with her husband and he is not studying, then she is permitted to sing.

The Covering of a Woman's Hair

A married woman's hair, like a woman's voice, is considered a possible lure to other men and thus is to be reserved for her own eyes and those of her husband. At all other times, she is required to cover it with a wig, scarf, or some other suitable device.

Hard Core Jewish Women

The Role of Jewish Women

Let's stop being judgmental over the role of Orthodox Jewish women. The feminist ideal of treating women as being completely interchangeable with men is incompatible with Judaism — it's not an egalitarian religion. Rather, all aspects of life and worship are compartmentalized into "what men do" and "what women do." Actions are viewed in terms of duties and obligations — the question of rights never arises. Orthodox Jewish women view themselves as having equal dignity with men, although that dignity is expressed through different social roles. The primary responsibility of men is in the synagogue, while women were assigned the roles of wife and caretaker for the home and children. Judaism has great respect for the importance of a wife's role, even if it seems slave-like and drudgery to the rest of us.

Home-life in Orthodox Judaism is a rich world of familial love, nurturing of others, prayer, intellect, and communal festivity. Many, if not all, of the chores homemakers do are themselves *mitzvot* (*Torah* obligations). Nourishing their families with the meals they cook is a *mitzvah*. Preparing food for *Shabbat* and the holidays takes on an additional spiritual dimension because it will be used in festive meals. Cleaning one's house creates an orderly environment which is conducive to inner clarity. Caring for the development of the Jewish souls of their children is a vital mitzvah that ensures the continuation of the Jewish People and tradition. Observant Jewish women take pride in the fact that their work is a holy service to *Hashem*. They do not view cooking, cleaning, and taking care of babies as mundane activities. Performing these chores are acts of worship and religious devotion, and allows Jewish women to elevate themselves and their households. [Whatever turns you on!]

Cooking is a very important and time-consuming task for any caretaker, yet it becomes especially difficult for the mother in an Orthodox Jewish family, due largely to the complex laws of *kashrut (See Section I, "A Guide for Sharing Space with an Observant Jew" Chapter)*. The women are responsible for making sure the entire family eats only *kosher* meals. This is part of their duty as guardians of the household. Kashrut laws not only make food preparation more involved; more importantly, they link food preparation intricately with religion. Sorting dishes, planning meals, washing vegetables — the preparation of every meal becomes a religious ritual because the work is done to fulfill God's laws.

Men Rule in Traditional Judaism

Original Torah law permits a man to have more than one wife (although it was considered extremely wrong to do so, unless truly necessary, such as when the first wife was barren), while a woman can have only one husband. Torah law also specifies that a man can divorce his wife against her will, (however the sages say that if he does so without true justification, he is hated by God), while a wife cannot divorce her husband without his permission.

There are many ways in which, according to the Torah, women are considered unequal with men. Traditional Judaism addresses the deity in the masculine gender, teaches that God's message was conveyed primarily through men such as Abraham and Moses, bestows the privilege of leadership upon men, and has traditionally excluded women from such central areas of religious expression as study and vocal participation in the synagogue. It places prohibitions upon menstruating and postpartum women and discriminates against women in matters of inheritance. Men write the prayers and make the laws. Women are not equal in social status; they are not given positions of authority. Moreover, although a husband is required to love his wife as himself and honor her more than himself (in physical matters) and not pain her even emotionally, he is nevertheless, the head of the house, and she is told to revere and, in most circumstances, follow him.

Orthodox synagogues are male-dominated because they are the physical center for male worship, socializing, and often study as well. Jewish law requires that men and women be separated during prayer. *Mechitzah* is the term used for a barrier that separates men and women or the designated areas of the synagogue that create sacred space for each gender to connect with Hashem without distraction. Torah scrolls and other holy objects are kept in the men's section. In many

Orthodox synagogues, probably due to lack of funds, the women's section is poorly climate controlled, and women cannot see (sometimes can't even hear!) what's going on in the men's section, where the services are being led. Women are not obligated by Jewish law to attend formal religious services, and cannot participate in many aspects of the services (traditional Jewish services have a very high degree of "audience participation" – and women cannot actively take part in running the service). Because of these issues, many Orthodox women rarely attend services. Devout men attend the synagogue one to three times a day.

According to *halacha*, there are three positive commandments for which women are held directly responsible: lighting the candles on sacred dates, baking bread for Sabbath, and complying with the family purity laws. Unlike men, women are exempted from all positive commandments ("thou shalts" as opposed to "thou shalt nots") that are time-sensitive (that is, commandments that must be performed at a specific time of the day or year), because the woman's duties as wife and mother are so important that they cannot be postponed to fulfill a commandment. In that exemption often translates into exclusion, women in effect become totally barred from participation in many religious rituals. Accordingly, women are regarded as less privileged than men. Every morning men thank God for "not making me a woman." The corresponding women's prayer, thanking God for making me "according to his will," is supposedly not a statement of resignation to a lower status. Rather, this prayer is to thank

God for making women closer than men to His idea of spiritual perfection, and for all the joys of being a woman generally. However, the combination of the exemption from fourteen commandments and separation during prayer often creates a perception by non-Observant people that women have an extremely inferior place in the synagogue. Ya think?

Laws of Family Purity

The Laws of Family Purity, as recorded in the Torah, prohibit a husband from having intercourse with his wife if she is menstruating. The woman is considered ritually impure (*niddah*) at that time. The Torah does not specify the reason for the laws of niddah, but then again, no reasons are given for any of the commandments. Separation of the spouses begins at the first sign of blood, and the minimum period of menstrual flow allowed is five days, even if the women just bleeds for one. *Talmudic* scholars, in years gone by, extended the period of separation for an additional seven days after the menstrual flow stops. [Thanks, guys.] Whereas the Bible prohibits intercourse, the Torah whizzes decided that a man should not share a bed or even touch his wife while she is ritually impure. This means that each month, spouses have a minimum of 12 days of separation. That's nearly half a month! Before the spouses can connect, the woman is required to visit the ritual bath called a *mikveh* to be ritually purified. If she and her husband violate the law, they are subject to arrest and punishment, not that this is enforced. Immersion in the mikveh symbolically reconnects one to the infinite and reminds us of our essential moral freedom and transcendent spiritual nature. It is an act of rebirth into the natural state of purity and clarity.

At the mikveh, the woman may not have anything between her and the water at any part of her body including jewelry and make-up. When she immerses, all of her must be touching water including her hair. The night a woman returns from the mikveh, she and her husband are required to have relations. [Who knows what God's punishment is for not making love that night, but why chance it?] Biologically speaking, the best night to conceive is usually mikveh night.

Another component of the Laws of Family Purity is a woman's status of *yoledet* (another form of ritual impurity). This begins when a women is in the later stages of labor and is unable to walk without assistance. The rules for a *yoledet* are similar to those of a niddah. An Observant Jewish husband cannot touch his wife, see her undressed, or look at her vagina when she is a yoledet. Some rabbis forbid the attendance of the husband in the delivery room to avert any violations of the Jewish law. Others maintain that a woman's need for support during childbirth outweighs this concern, and thus the husband may (and perhaps should) attend.

After childbirth, the woman is still considered ritually unclean or yoledet while she is bleeding vaginally. If the woman delivers a boy baby, she remains yoledet for a minimum of seven days and on the eighth day the boy is circumcised. For a girl baby, yoledet lasts a minimum of two weeks. Even if a baby is stillborn, the husband is still not permitted to physically touch his wife in order to provide her with comfort. This also holds true if she miscarries after more than about seven weeks' gestation. While the woman is yoledet, she can not even hand the baby to the husband. Instead the baby has to be put down and then the husband can pick the baby up. Seven days after the yoledet ends, the woman must immerse herself in the mikveh and then she is officially decontaminated.

The Torah considers a woman who has recently delivered a baby to have a similar status as a sick person in mortal danger. For the first three days after birth, one may desecrate the Sabbath for her sake if she requires something, whether she asks for it or not. From the fourth to seventh day, one may violate the Sabbath at the woman's request.

Sex During Pregnancy

Sexual relations are fully permitted during pregnancy. Moreover, the husband's obligation to his wife to have relations at regular intervals is not waived during pregnancy, without the wife's consent. In fact, the Talmud even mentions that relations from the second trimester on have a positive effect on the baby, although this in itself does not constitute an obligation.

Modesty (Tsneis)

Tsneis is a style of dress and behavior for both men and women, both of which emphasize modesty. Tsneis is part of a triumvirate of daily Jewish life, which also includes *Kedushah* (holiness), and *Taharah* (purity). Observant Jews believe that if they retain these three qualities in their daily lives, their reward will be significant in the World To Come (the Jewish version of heaven). [But what about this life – there's no way they're having as much fun as those of us on the dark side.]

Judaism strikes a balance by acknowledging the need for both physical and non-physical self-expression. Sensuality is channeled into the intimate aspects of one's married life, where it is affirmed and encouraged as a means of expressing one's deepest self to the other. It is simultaneously held back from the public eye, where it will inevitably create distortion and superficiality in how one is perceived. Jewish law permits a woman to display only those parts of her that convey her essence — her intellect, her emotions, and her individuality. She is forbidden to be inappropriately alluring or noticeable. Dress such as spaghetti strap tank tops, short skirts, and low necklines encourage the casual observer to focus on the body and not on the mind or the soul of the woman so attired. Publicly projecting oneself in such a way has the severe spiritual consequence of banishing God's presence. Modest dress, on the other hand, not only prevents men from viewing women as objects, but, more importantly, allows women themselves to internalize a spiritual self-image. The Jewish People believe that a woman's sense of self and power should not come from the number of heads she can turn, but rather from the minds and hearts she can turn. [I don't know how realistic that is, but whatever.]

The clothing worn by Hard Core Jewish Women is not supposed to cling to them or be revealing in any way, but they don't have to be formless. The clothes also don't have to be dark and dreary. I have lots of fun buying cute and very stylish clothes that are also respectful of the Jewish People so I can dress properly when I need to. One does not have to be frumpy to be modest. In front the clothing must reach up to the collar bone and to just below the nape of the neck in the back. Any exposed part of the leg should be covered with stockings. Long sleeves that cover the elbow are required. [I never knew that elbows are considered sexy or alluring.] Women should wear dresses or skirts (without slits), but not pants. If a Jewish woman happens to attract attention for the length of her skirt or for wearing long sleeves on a warm day, that's okay for she is displaying her modesty and dignity and desire to do what is right in God's eyes.

Wearing Wigs

Then there's the issue of a woman covering her hair. According to Jewish law, a woman's hair is one of her most beautiful aspects and, as such, a married woman does not expose her hair to public view. Only a woman's husband is permitted to see her hair. The Hard Cores believe that this aids in increasing the intimacy between a husband and wife when she, so to speak, "lets her hair down." Some women prefer to cover their heads with scarves or hats. However, as a matter of fashion and a desire to blend in, most of them choose to wear wigs. When a wig is worn by a Jewish woman for religious reasons, it is called a *sheitel*.

Sex and the Jewish People

Forget About the Hole in the Sheet Rumor

Forget about "the hole in the sheet" caricature of nookie Jewish-style. It's completely inaccurate because Jewish teachings place importance on the "closeness of flesh", instructing that the husband and wife should have sex fully naked, but under a sheet and preferably with the lights off. Modesty has always been an important quality in Judaism. A woman who insists on not being naked gives her husband grounds to divorce her. Regarding where "the hole in the sheet" notion might have come from, some think that Rabbi Halafta, a Jewish sage, introduced the concept to reconcile two conflicting statements in the Bible. Deuteronomy 25:5 commands a man to take his brother's childless widow as his wife, but Leviticus 18:16 forbids a man to see his brother's wife naked. Others suggest a more modern reason for the fallacy: that people saw duvet covers with a central hole drying on the line in Orthodox neighborhoods and let their minds run wild.

Judaism Values Sex

Judaism values sex and encourages the enjoyment and pleasuring of the partners in a relationship. A woman can actually divorce her husband if she does not feel sexually satisfied by their relationship. A man has a duty to give his wife sex regularly and to ensure that sex is pleasurable for her. He is also obligated to watch for signs that his wife wants sex, and to offer it to her without her having to ask for it. The woman's right to sexual intercourse is referred to as *onah,* and is one of a wife's basic rights which a husband may not reduce. The *Talmud* specifies both the quantity and quality of sex that a man must give his wife. It details the frequency of sexual obligation based on the husband's occupation, although this obligation can be modified in the *ketubah* (marriage contract). For example, the wife of a man of independence is entitled to sex every day, should she wish it, while a lowly mule-driver is obligated to satisfy his wife just once a week.

In Jewish law, sex is not considered shameful, sinful, or obscene. When sexual desire is satisfied between a husband and wife at the proper time, out of mutual love and desire, sex is considered a special holy *mitzvah.* The creation stories in the *Torah* suggest two purposes of sexual activity. The first and most obvious is procreation. Sex is part of God's plan for populating the world; it fulfills God's will for both animals and humans. The second purpose of sexual relations is companionship, which the Torah seems to regard as an even greater justification for sexual relations than procreation. In Jewish tradition, the belief that "it is not good for man to be alone" is as important, if not more important, than the commandment to "be fruitful and multiply."

Sex between a husband and wife is permitted (even recommended) at times when conception is impossible, such as when the woman is pregnant, after menopause, or when the woman is using a permissible form of contraception. Although some sources take a more narrow view, the general view of *halacha* is that any sexual act that does not involve *sh'chatat zerah* (destruction of seed, that is, ejaculation outside the vagina) is permissible. As one passage in the Talmud states, "a man may do whatever he pleases with his wife." In fact, there are passages in the Talmud that encourage foreplay to arouse the woman. Whoa! Those Jewish guys can be wild sometimes. In principle, birth control is permitted, so long as the couple is committed to eventually fulfilling the *mitzvah* to be fruitful and multiply (which, at a minimum, consists of having two children, one of each gender). The type of birth control used must not destroy the seed or block the passage of the seed. That rules out condoms, diaphragms, and IUDs but the pill is perfectly acceptable under Jewish law.

What Kind of Love-Making is Allowed?

Rabbinical scholars are not always of one mind when it comes to which positions are kosher for the bedroom. Some Talmudic rabbis are opposed to "overturning the table" but *Maimonides* asserted that a husband "may kiss any organ he wishes. And he may have intercourse in a natural or unnatural manner as long as he does not expend semen to no purpose." Not surprisingly, the Hard Cores have other specific requirements for lovemaking. Sex should only be experienced in a time of joy. Sex for selfish personal satisfaction, without regard for the partner's pleasure is wrong and evil. A couple may not have sexual relations while drunk or quarreling. [But what about Kathleen Turner's question to Danny DeVito in 'War of the Roses' when she asked: "Have you ever made angry love?" And Danny responded, "Is there any other kind?"] Sex may never be used as a weapon or a form of punishment against a spouse, either by depriving the spouse of sex or by compelling it. It is a serious offense to use sex (or lack thereof) to punish or manipulate a spouse. A man may not take a vow to abstain from sex for an extended period of time, and may not take a journey for an extended period of time, because that would deprive his wife of sexual relations. In addition, a husband's consistent refusal to engage in sexual relations is grounds for compelling a man to <u>divorce</u> his wife, even if the couple has already fulfilled the halachic obligation to procreate. If a woman withholds sex from her husband, the husband may divorce her without paying the substantial divorce settlement provided for in the <u>ketubah.</u>

The "Hurt-Me, Hurt-Me" Mentality

You need to be somewhat of a masochist if you want to be an Observant Jew. The Jewish People believe that nothing occurs by chance and if something bad happens, God wanted it to happen. Suffering is an inextricable part of the process of redemption for their sins. Moreover, pain and suffering are considered necessary to keep them on the right path. Hard Cores believe that when things are going too well, it is human nature to take life for granted. Trauma, on the other-hand, brings them to the edges of life, allowing them to view it from a new and revealing angle. *Torah*-true Jews feel that it is important to view pain as a test that examines how consumed one is with material comfort as opposed to spiritual growth. Instead of being broken by pain, they are commanded to demonstrate their complete trust in God by continuing their lives with an intense commitment to goodness, thereby challenging God to live up to His promises of being righteous and fair.

Even in the deepest moments of despair like the Holocaust, the Jewish People's unwavering faith in Hashem gives them the capacity to accept pain as part of the challenge of life. Some Observant Jews in Auschwitz risked their lives to pay homage to Hashem by lighting the *Shabbat* candles, having a baby boy circumcised, or having a Bar Mitzvah ceremony for a young man. Despite their setbacks, despite their confusion, despite their pain, they remained absolutely confident that goodness would prevail. After the Holocaust, Rebbetzin

Tzila Sorotzkin, a noted teacher in a Jewish seminary for women in Krakow, said: "I do not regret the end of the ordeals and hardships I experienced in Auschwitz. I am grateful to Hashem for relieving me of them. I pray that I and my People may never again be subjected to such trials. Instead, may Hashem give us a taste of the final days, when we will experience everlasting true joy and peace."

Observant Jews are taught to trust God's supreme love and care for their welfare. They believe that everything God does is for their own benefit. Even if Jews are being good doobies and living a Torah life, they may still be punished if the rest of the world doesn't follow suit. Because they were chosen by God to serve as an example for the rest of the world, Jews are responsible for the sins of all mankind. [No one ever said that life was fair or easy.]

Some Observant Jews believe that suffering is caused by a weakness in one's devotion to God. Generally, it is believed that God gave humans free will to feel pleasure and pain, and His purpose in allowing deep suffering of the innocent must be good, even if mysterious. God suffers along with the sufferer. Some Jews (e.g. the *Hasidim* or "black hats") believe that suffering is punishment for past-life sins. Knowing why God allows suffering is not as important as knowing that God will punish the perpetrators.

Sometimes tragedies challenge even the most pious Jews in understanding and accepting that it is the work of God. But their faith and trust in God's goodness eases the pain. A good example of this was the suicide bombing on August 19, 2002 of the Number 2 bus in Jerusalem. It was filled with mostly ultra-Orthodox Jewish families returning home after praying at the Western Wall. Seven of the 20 people who died were children. While the rabbis tried to encourage their congregants to not over-analyze or philosophize about the situation and just try to be better Jews, even the ultra-Orthodox needed to find an explanation for the merciless killing of children. "Why would God allow such a thing to happen to us? We're Torah-true Jews and living exactly the way God wants us to." Some people from the community finally came up with the explanation that it required the death of innocents to make up for the extreme sins of the Israeli people. They attributed the cruelness of the catastrophe to immodest behavior by the people of Israel. The violent act occurred during a three-week period in the summer when the ultra-Orthodox enjoy the summer and go to the beach. There, many immodest behaviors occur including men and women not swimming separately. By finding an explanation that consoled them, these members of the community were able to move forward and put their trust in God.

No Gossip Allowed (Loshon Hora)

Loshon Hora (LA-shun HOE-rah); derogatory gossip or slander) is considered by the Jewish People to be one of the worst sins imaginable. They don't like people spreading around smut or saying things that might hurt someone's feeling. To ensure that no one inadvertently violates the law, Torah scholars embellished the Torah-prescribed mitzvah over the years, resulting in the following loshon hora rules:

- You are forbidden to relate derogatory gossip to a single individual or to a group.

- You are not even allowed to repeat well-known derogatory gossip about someone.

- Even if you would relate derogatory gossip if the subject were present, it is still forbidden for you to repeat this loshon hora to others.

- Speaking loshon hora about someone in his/her presence is a grave sin, even if your sole intention in mentioning the person's faults is for constructive criticism. Such an action could cause an individual humiliation and mortification. Thus, corrective comments should be delivered privately.

- Even if you have a passion for the truth and that the truth be known, you are forbidden to say that a person did something improper. Although your words might be meant totally without malice, they still constitute loshon hora. You are allowed to relate details of an improper action only if it is constructive.

- If you see an Observant Jew violate a mitzvah (commandment) repeatedly, you are obligated to judge him favorably and are forbidden to tell others that he has sinned. Perhaps he did not know that the action was prohibited and therefore he repeated it many times. Or perhaps he did not realize the severity of his transgression.

What's the Big Deal About Torah?

God put the Tree of Knowledge of good and evil in the Garden of Eden to give Adam and Eve a choice – to obey Him or disobey Him. Adam and Eve were free to do anything they wanted, except eat from the Tree of Knowledge of good and evil. In Genesis 2:16-17 it says, "And the LORD God commanded the man, 'You are free to eat from any tree in the garden; but you must not eat from the tree of knowledge of good and evil, for when you eat of it you will surely die.'" Why did God tempt them by putting the Tree of Knowledge within their reach? It's all about free will and making the right choice in the face of temptation. That is what the Jewish People believe leads to achievement and the "ultimate self-realization." (aish.com)

Satan tempted Eve and she ate the forbidden fruit from the Tree of Knowledge in order to be like God. Then she had Adam take a bite. Bad Eve – she disobeyed God's orders. Some believe that Adam and Eve were created with no evil inside of them. Their disobedience resulted in a change in man's nature to include an evil inclination, along with an inclination toward goodness. Many believe that wrongdoing results from God-given free will plus the urge to satisfy personal needs, which could result in wrong choices.

God gave the *Torah* to the Jews so they would know how to behave as spiritual beings. It's a roadmap that guides Hard Cores in living the way God wants them to. There are 613 commandments (obligations / Jewish laws / *mitzvot*) included in the Torah that govern such areas as philanthropy, sacrifices, prayer, ritual purity, dietary laws, and observances of the *Sabbath* and other holy days. The Torah's basic theme is Love Your Fellow Man As Yourself. Orthodox Jews believe that if they lead a proper religious life, they will find happiness and fulfillment. Praying and following Torah law is their purpose for existence. By doing what God wants them to do, they feel closer to God and that gives them great pleasure by enriching their lives with "true contentment and peace." They believe that the pain and discomfort of "doing the right thing" is the price they pay for spiritual pleasure. The Hebrew word for this sort of experience is *bitul*, a *Hassidic* concept that true happiness comes not from what one does, but by focusing on what has been given to him or her in life. Happiness is not achieved by focusing on one's own self-worth or one's achievements. They are all temporary and the pleasures felt by an accomplishment fade over time. But getting close to God and following His guidelines for living brings lasting pleasure. [From my perspective, God's roadmap is too strict, too serious, not any fun, and life is too short to be obsessed about following a set of rules and regulations that often don't make any sense in the contemporary world. That's why I continue to live on the dark side.]

Torah Whizzes Have Power

The *Torah* encourages Jews to unquestioningly rely on the leadership and judgment of gedolim (singular is gadol), who are great religious leaders, rabbis, prophets, and sages. Gedolim possess profound insight into Torah and their interpretations of the Torah make it comprehensible and meaningful to the common Jew. The Jewish People assume that everything they are told by a gadol is proper and true. The Torah's directive not to stray from the teachings of the Priests or Levites and judge either to the right or left is interpreted in the Talmud to mean: "Even if they tell you that right is left, you should follow their advice." If perchance something they are told seems incorrect, many Observant Jews dare not challenge it, since "Who are we to question?" By clinging to the gadol and following his exemplary qualities and behavior, the Jewish People behave as God wants them to and they feel closer to Him. [But aren't gedolim mortals and therefore not all-knowing? It doesn't matter.] According to aish.com, "one must carefully study and trust the words and writings of our prophets and sages. Belief in our great religious leaders, who are the shepherds of our faith, is equated with belief in God Himself."

The Jewish People view gedolim as experts in all areas of life. For example, it is simply assumed that anyone who is an expert in *halacha* (Torah law) is qualified to be a marriage counselor, as if expertise in the latter field is magically imparted to a Torah scholar after he reaches a certain level. Torah study certainly can imbue people with insight into other areas of life. But rabbis must have the integrity, humility, and intellectual honesty to say "I don't know", "This is not my area of expertise, but here are my thoughts", or "Let me refer you to someone who is better qualified to deal with your issue."

A good example of misguided advice from gedolim that caused deaths was during WWII. According to Efraim Zuroff, Director of the Israel Office of the Simon Wiesenthal Centre, "You won't hear this spoken about much by Orthodox Jews." During WWII, more than 20 Eastern Europe *yeshivot* (plural of yeshiva) escaped the Holocaust, but only the Mir Yeshiva was rescued in its entirety. Sugihard Sempo, the Japanese consul in 1940, issued transit visas to about 6,000 Jewish refugees from both Poland and Lithuania. The visas allowed the fleeing Jews to take the Trans Siberian railway to Vladivostok, and to sail from there to Japan. The heads of the yeshiva (roshei) of that time advised their students that if they sought Soviet exit visas, the entire yeshiva would be deported to Siberia. "In some cases, the roshei who gave the advice to reject the visas did not themselves need it because they already had visas to America." Only the Mir Yeshiva defied the gadol's advice and obtained the exit permits and visas in an organized fashion. That is why they were able to survive intact.

Mechanically following the advice of a mortal when the advice seems inappropriate sounds ignorant. Can it be that

God wants mankind to adhere to something that is intuitively wrong? Don't we need to fight complacency and use the thinking portion of our brains if we believe that someone's advice is wrong? As Isaac Bashevis Singer once said, "A voice from heaven should be ignored if it is not on the side of justice."

Jewish Rituals and Holidays

Jewish Rituals

For Jews, religious observances are a way of turning beliefs into actions. These actions are the rituals that create religious moments in a person's everyday life. There are several major Jewish rituals that mark the passage of time and make time holy, other rituals are directed at helping a person to "think" Jewishly, and still other rituals are designed to help Jews to act Jewishly. The rituals that divide time and make time holy include the holy days and the special celebrations that are a part of the life cycle of the Jew. The most important religious rituals in Judaism include keeping the *Sabbath*, circumcision, Bar Mitzvah, wedding, and burial prayers.

Keeping Hashem Top-of-Mind

Hard Core Jewish People use all kinds of reminders to keep *Hashem* top-of-mind every waking moment. The Jewish laws commanding these rituals come from a passage in the Torah called the *Shema* (shuh-MA). In that passage, God commands the Jewish People to keep His words constantly in their minds and in their hearts. The rituals keep them on track and point them in the direction their lives should follow. These reminders include the following:

Mezuzah (meh-ZUZ-ah): On the doorposts (frames of the doors) of Observant and non-Observant Jewish homes, there is often a small case commonly known as a mezuzah. The mezuzah is not, as some suppose, a good-luck charm, nor does it have any connection with the lamb's blood placed on the doorposts in Egypt. Rather, it serves as a constant reminder of God's presence and God's *mitzvot* (commandments). Inside the case is a scroll with the words of the Shema that must be handwritten in a special style of writing. Then the mezuzah is affixed to the doorpost with a special prayer, of course. Every time the Jewish People pass through a door with a mezuzah on it, they touch the mezuzah and then kiss the fingers that touched it, expressing love and respect for God and His mitzvot.

Tallit (TOLL-it; also pronounced tallis): This is a prayer shawl worn for morning prayer during the week as well as on Shabbat and other holy days. The rectangular-shaped shawl has special fringes, called *tzitzit,* on each of the four corners. To satisfy the mitzvah of wearing fringes on the corners of their garments, some men opt to wear a tallis rather than *tzitzit.* In Orthodox Jewish communities, a male Jew who has reached the age of 13 wears a tallit and/or tzitzit to remind the wearer of his religious obligations.

Tefillin (tuh-FILL-in): The Torah commands the Jewish People to bind the words of God to their hands and between their eyes. They do this by "laying tefillin" which involves binding to their arms and foreheads a small black laquered box containing scrolls of Torah passages. Among Observant

Jews, wearing tefillin is a mitzvah of the greatest significance. Tefillin are meant to remind the Hard Cores of God's commandments. At weekday morning synagogue services, one case is tied to the arm, with the scrolls at the biceps and leather straps which hold it in place extending down the arm to the hand, then another case is tied to the head, with the case on the forehead and the straps hanging down over the shoulders. Appropriate blessings are recited during this process. The tefillin are removed at the conclusion of the morning services. The scrolls in tefillin must be hand-written in a special style of writing. Carter's set of "perfect" tefillin cost us $1,200, but inferior models can be purchased for a lot less. Fortunately, if properly cared for, tefillin will last a lifetime.

Tzitzit (TSIT-see): Another Torah commandment is for guys to wear tzitzit (fringes) at the corners of their garments as a reminder of all the other mitzvot (commandments), and to aid in steering them away from their earthly motivations to a greater connection with God. Traditional Jews, like Carter, wear a garment, called a tzitzit, which is specifically made to have four corners so that the mitzvah can be fulfilled. Carter wears his tzitzit under his clothing with the fringes hanging out. On the cover of this book, you can see Carter's fringes hanging over the top of his bathing suit. Some people wear the fringes concealed.

Kippa (KEEP-puh;): A kippa is another word for yarmulke, skull cap, or head cover. Wearing a kippa is a Jewish custom and an outward symbol that one is trying to live as a good

Jew. The kippa shows respect for God, separates man from God, and it serves as a reminder of Jewish law and tradition.

Jewish Holidays

Jews celebrate seven major holidays / festivals each year which include Rosh Hashanah (New Year), the Day of Atonement (Yom Kippur), the feast of Tabernacles (Sukkot), and Passover with its ceremonial family meal, the *Seder*. All of the holidays begin the evening before the date specified on most calendars. This is because a Jewish "day" begins and ends at sunset, rather than at midnight. Most of the holidays require at least one major feast, and preparing food is permitted on these days. Naturally the responsibility for the feast belongs to the lady of the household. This involves planning, shopping, and slaving in the kitchen unless one can afford to hire help.

If you go by the Jewish calendar, Jewish holidays actually occur on the same day every year. Unlike the calendar most of us use, the Jewish calendar is tied to the moon's cycles instead of the Earth's passage around the sun. The Jewish calendar loses about 11 days relative to the Gregorian (solar) calendar every year, but makes up for it by adding an extra "leap" month every two or three years. As a result, the holidays don't always fall on the same solar day, but they always fall within the same month or two.

The Jewish month of Tishri, which falls during the months of September and October on the Gregorian calendar, is probably the busiest time of the year for Jewish holidays and the peak opportunity for Jewish women to have nervous breakdowns. During this period, there are a total of thirteen days of special religious significance, seven of them holidays on which work is not permitted but slaving in the kitchen is: Rosh Hashanah, Yom Kippur, and the first and second days of Sukkot: Shemini Atzeret (the last day of Sukkot), and Simchat Torah. By work, this means the same things that are prohibited on Shabbat except that cooking, baking, transferring fire, and carrying, all of which are forbidden on Shabbat, are permitted on holidays. When a holiday occurs on Shabbat, the full Shabbat restrictions are observed. For Hard Core Jewish Women, they are stretched to the max at this time of the year with an onslaught of special meal preparations. Moreover, they are commanded to perform their role with joy, which has got to be a challenge at times. [Hopefully there are special happy pills they can take to get themselves through it.]

Rosh HaShanah (September or October) – The Jewish New Year marks the beginning of a 10-day period of prayer, self-examination, and repentance, which culminates on the fast of Yom Kippur. These 10 days are referred to as the Days of Awe or the High Holy Days. Rosh Hashanah is a happy, festive holiday. The common greeting at this time is L'shanah tovah ("for a good year"). No work is allowed.

Yom Kippur (September or October) - Yom Kippur is the Jewish Day of Atonement, a day of fasting and repentance for Jews to reconcile themselves with God for mistakes made in the last year. No work can be performed on that day and Jews are supposed to refrain from eating and drinking (even water) for 25 hours. The punishment for disregarding the prohibition against eating or drinking is "Karet," premature death at the hand of God. Some less well known restrictions for this holiday that are specified in the Talmud include: not washing or bathing, no cosmetics or deodorants, no leather shoes, and no sexual relations.

Sukkot (late September or October) – Pronounced SUE-coat, this joyful holiday commemorates the forty-year period during which the children of Israel were wandering in the desert, living in temporary shelters. Known as the festival of booths, Observant Jews have a temporary shelter or *sukkah* (SOOK-ah) constructed in their yards and they eat and sleep in it. The holiday begins four days after Yom Kippur and lasts for eight days. No work is permitted on the first or second days.

Shemini Atzeret – This is the eighth or final day of Sukkot. No work is permitted.

Simchat Torah (October) – This holiday occurs the day after Shemini Atzeret and means "Rejoicing in the Torah." Each week in the synagogue, Observant Jews publicly read a few chapters from the Torah, starting with Genesis Chapter 1 and working their way through to Deuteronomy 34. On Simchat

Torah, the last Torah portion is read. This completion of the readings is a time of great celebration. There are processions around the synagogue carrying Torah scrolls and plenty of high-spirited singing and dancing in the synagogue with the Torahs. Drinking is also common during this time. No work is permitted on this day.

Chanukah (late-November or December) – Also known as the festival of lights, this holiday commemorates the rededication of the Temple in Jerusalem after a successful revolt against the Selucid Greeks. The victorious Jews needed to light the Temple's menorah (candelabra over the ark containing the Torah), but they had only enough oil to last for one day. It would take eight days to prepare more oil. Miraculously, the one-day supply of oil lasted for eight days, keeping the menorah lit continuously. This phenomenon is commemorated with the lighting of candles in a menorah for eight nights. Gift-giving is not a traditional part of the holiday, but it adds more festivity to the holiday.

Purim (late February or March) – This is one of the times that the Jewish People can rock out. Purim is one of the most joyous and fun holidays on the Jewish calendar. The holiday, which lasts one day, celebrates the rescue of the Jews from a Hitler-like person named Hamon (HAY-mon), who was hell-bent on genocide. Jews are commanded to eat, drink profusely, and be merry. Although work is technically not forbidden on this holiday, some Jews prefer not to work on it because of a rabbinical dictum that no good will come from work done on this day. This makes sense since Jews are instructed to drink enough on that day that they don't know the difference between Mordecai (the good guy) and Hamon (the bad guy). Naturally, so that the Jewish People don't let it all hang out and completely forget about *Hashem*, the primary commandment related to Purim is to hear the reading of the book of Esther.

Passover (late March or April) – This holiday lasts eight days for Jews outside of Israel (seven days within Israel) and commemorates the Exodus of the Jews from Egypt. Strictly Observant Jews do not work, go to school, or carry out any business on the first two and last two days of Passover. Preparing for this holiday at home is so oppressive that many Observant Jews flee their homes and go to a hotel or take a cruise that is Kosher for Passover *(See Section I, "A Guide for Sharing Space With an Observant Jew" Chapter)*. No *chametz* (HUM-metz) or food that is made of grain and water is consumed. Instead, unleavened bread or matzah is eaten. The Jewish People not only refrain from eating these grains, but they use a special set of cooking and eating utensils to prepare Passover meals. Nothing can be used for cooking during Passover that was used at any other time unless it is first *kashered*. The entire house has to be scrupulously cleaned to remove any traces of crumbs or grains that might violate Passover requirements. Many women surpass even these expectations. It's not enough just to get the bread out of the house or set aside so they don't have access to it. They clean the vacuum cleaner filter to ensure it doesn't have any chametz in it; they clean the seal around the refrigerator door; they clean the windows. While not required, this extra cleaning is a socially established way for a woman to demonstrate her piety and dedication to her religion. Spring cleaning becomes an act of devotion.

Shavu'ot (May or June) - Commemorates the giving of the Torah to the Jews at Mt. Sinai. Work is not permitted on this holiday, which lasts for one day in Israel and two days everywhere else. For Observant Jews, it is customary to stay up the entire night of Shavu'ot and study Torah, and then pray as early as possible in the morning.

Tisha B'Av (late July or August) - The Fast of the Ninth of Av (Av is one of the months in the Jewish calendar) is a day of mourning to commemorate the many tragedies that have befallen the Jewish people, many of which coincidentally have occurred on the Ninth of Av. *(See Section II, "Praying and Fasting" Chapter)*

Tu B'Shevat (late January or February) - Also known as the New Year for Trees, there are few customs or observances related to this holiday. One custom is to eat a new fruit or plant trees on this day.

Praying and Fasting

Why Do They Pray All the Time?

Recitation of prayers is the central characteristic of Jewish worship because God commands them to be aware of Him at all times. Observant Jews are commanded to pray three times daily (morning, noon, and night) and more on *Shabbat* and Jewish holidays. If they don't follow that commandment, Hard Cores truly believe that bad things may happen to them in the World To Come, and that would be a bummer. *(See Section II, "The Messiah and the World To Come" Chapter)* The simple act of uttering a blessing has profound implications including: (1) an acknowledgement of the existence of God; (2) an admission that what is in this world comes from God; and (3) an act of submission to the will of God.

Proper concentration is considered essential for prayer and there are certain prayers that are invalid if recited without the required awareness and intention. [That must be a real drag to have one's prayer invalidated.] In addition to the three times daily prayers, Orthodox Jews also say a prayer to *Hashem* for all acts of loving-kindness that He bestows upon them including: when they wake up in the morning, before having a glass of water, after using the bathroom, upon smelling fragrant woods, when putting on a new garment, buying a new house, upon witnessing lightning, seeing falling stars, at the sight of a rainbow, and for multitudes of other events. This enables them to bring spirituality and holiness to every place they might be including their excursions into and involvements with that which is mundane. It's always fun being in the middle of a conversation with Carter when he's home for a visit and he starts saying a prayer before taking a drink of water. [Whatever!]

Jewish prayer involves all the physical senses in an effort to draw the worshiper in, body and soul. There are garments which are worn specifically for prayer and there is a complex choreography to Jewish prayer. *(See Section II, "Jewish Rituals and Holidays: Keeping Hashem Top-of-Mind" Chapter)* Jewish prayer involves movement. Some prayers are said standing, while others may be recited while seated. Often worshipers will sway to the rhythm of their own prayers, but this isn't required. There are times when the worshiper kisses the *tzitzit* (fringes), times when he rises up on his toes in imitation of the angels in heaven, and times when he stands perfectly still. Jewish prayer involves music in many forms. Most of the service is chanted. There are many prayers which are sung to congregational tunes.

Why Are They Always Fasting?

According to the renowned *Maimonides* in his <u>Jewish Law Code</u>, the aim of Jewish fast days is to "awaken the hearts towards repentance; to recall to us, both the evil deeds of our fathers, and our own evil deeds, which caused anguish to befall both them and us and thereby to cause us to return towards the good." Additionally, by refraining from eating, one is humbled and more appreciative of the dependence of humanity on God.

<u>The seven fast days include</u>:

- <u>Yom Kippur</u>, the Day of Atonement, is the most holy day of the Jewish year. This is the only one of the fasts that was commanded in the Written Torah. One has to abstain from eating from sundown to sundown. In addition to not eating or drinking, Jews are not supposed to wash or shower, wear leather shoes, use ointments or perfumes, make love, or partake in other physical pleasures.

- <u>Tisha B'Av</u>, the Fast of the Ninth of <u>Av</u>, is a day of mourning to commemorate the multitudes of tragedies that have befallen the Jewish People, many of which coincidentally have occurred on the Ninth of Av. The prohibitions on Tisha B'Av itself are similar to those of Yom Kippur but it also includes the stringency of being only allowed to study certain portions of the Torah and Talmud. It is also forbidden to greet friends or acquaintances on Tisha B'Av. However, if greeted first, one should answer, but in a low tone in order not to arouse resentment. Yom Kippur and Tishah B'Av are the only fasts observed from sunset to sunset. All other fasts are from sunrise to sunset.

There are four public fast days that commemorate stages in the destruction of the first and second Temples, and Israel's expulsion from their homeland. These fasts are from sunrise to sunset and include:

- The Fast of the Firstborn is observed only by firstborn males on the day before Passover to commemorate the fact they were saved from the plague of the firstborn in Egypt.

- The Fast of the 17th of Tammuz (in June or July) commemorates the many calamities that have befallen the Jewish People on this day.

- The Tenth of Tevet (in December or January), is a minor fast day historically tied in with a whole chain of calamities which culminated in the destruction of the First Ancient Temple. The purpose of the fast is mourning and repentence. In the State of Israel, *kaddish* (the Jewish prayer for the deceased), is recited on this day for people whose date or place of death is unknown. Consequently, many rabbis have designated it as a day of remembrance for the Holocaust.

- The Fast of Esther (in February or March on the day before Purim) is a celebration fast in memory of the fast observed that day by all of Israel. On that very day, the enemies of the Jews had planned to subjugate and destroy them. The Jews went on a hunger strike, fasting and praying to God, and they were the victors. *(See Section II, "Jewish Rituals and Holidays: Purim" Chapter)*

* The time period between the 17th of Tammuz and the Ninth of Av referred to as the "Three Weeks", was designated by a highly esteemed Jewish Torah scholar as the time span into which to concentrate all mourning for calamities that befell the Jewish people over the centuries. Technically the Jewish People could mourn on a daily basis because so many dreadful things have happened to the Jews over the centuries. However, this would be a violation of Torah law because the mission of Observant Jews is to serve Hashem and fulfill His commandments with joy. If one is constantly mourning, it's kind of difficult to be joyful. Thus mourning for the historical tragedies is compacted into this three week period. The prohibitions during the Three Weeks include:

Visiting cinemas, theaters, concert halls or any other place where there is public entertainment is strictly prohibited. One has to keep their joyfulness down to a low roar.

With the exception of socks and undergarments, new clothes should not be purchased.

Haircuts and shaving are forbidden. According to some authorities, men who shave daily for business reasons may shave during this period.

No building or performing alterations in one's home is allowed, unless the work is important repair work. This prohibition includes painting, wall papering, and other forms of home decorations.

The restrictions below only apply for nine days of the three week period:

No eating meat or drinking wine, except on Shabbat.

Giving clothing to or getting clothing back from the cleaners or doing laundry is not permitted. Children's clothing, especially babies and infants, may be cleaned during this period. Also, this restriction doesn't apply to clothing worn directly against the body which requires frequent changing.

Weaving, knitting, and needle craft work, with the exception of repairing torn clothing, is prohibited during this period.

Swimming and bathing for pleasure is prohibited. Taking a bath or shower for hygiene purposes is permitted. Children in camp may go swimming during the instructional swim period. When necessary, visiting a *mikveh* is permitted.

Observing the Sabbath

Shabbat is considered the most important ritual observance in Judaism — even more important than Yom Kippur. People like me, who do not observe Shabbat, think of it as a day filled with stifling restrictions or as a day of prayer. But for those who observe Shabbat, it is a precious gift from God, a day of great joy eagerly awaited throughout the week, a time when they can set aside all of their weekday concerns and devote themselves to higher pursuits including prayer, study, good food, rest, and time spent with family and friends. By setting aside one day each week to imitate God in the manner of Shabbat rest, they are reminded of how important it is to act in a godly manner the other six days of the week. The Sabbath begins at 18 minutes before sundown on Friday evening, and Observant Jews are required for the next 25 hours to rest so they can return to their work with a sense of purpose and direction.

The lady of the house is in charge of seeing to it that all the Shabbat food is prepared and cooked before Shabbat arrives, the electric or gas stove remains on to heat food up on Saturday, the table is set with fresh linen and sparkling silver, with wine and *challot* (special Shabbat breads, the plural of *challah*), and the Shabbat candles are ready to be lit.

The laws of Shabbat as they developed are extensive and complex, but the essence remains the same: to provide a day for the community to live in imitation of God in order to remind people of their potential and purpose. No work is permitted on the Sabbath. Making love with one's spouse, taking a nap, heating up food on a Shabbat stove, serving food, and washing dishes are perfectly acceptable. None of those tasks are considered work. The term "work" in the Torah refers to *melachah* or the kind of work that is creative or that exercises control over one's environment. A total of 39 forms of "work" are forbidden, including:

- No squeezing or selecting fruit
- No kneading, grinding, or mashing
- No appliances may be turned on or off
- Unless one lives in an *eruv* (this refers to a fence — either real or symbolic — that surrounds a Jewish neighborhood, permitting carrying within its boundaries), Observant Jews cannot carry anything on the Sabbath. This includes a keychain, handkerchief, wallet, etc. The only things one may carry outdoors are things that are actually worn. [I wonder what the Jewish People who don't live in an eruv do when their noses are running on the Sabbath if they can't carry a pack of tissues.]
- No striking a match, using a telephone, starting a car, or even smoking a cigarette is permitted on the Sabbath.
- A flame may not be reduced or extinguished. If your house is on fire, leave it. You don't want God to punish you, do you?
- No writing of any kind is permitted, including drawing, typing, using a rubber stamp, calculations, taking measurements, gambling, or the playing of games of chance.

- No erasing or destroying of any form of writing
- No tearing of clothing or any kind of papers including toilet paper is allowed. The Hard Cores tear the toilet paper in advance of the Sabbath or use tissues.
- No planting or gardening
- No cooking: The Jewish People have an obligation to enhance the joy and festivity of the Sabbath with warm, abundant food, but they are not allowed to turn on a stove or oven on Shabbat. Instead they prepare dishes which can slowly cook overnight from Friday afternoon until Saturday noon, when the family returns from synagogue to enjoy Sabbath lunch. Another means of getting around the restriction is with the use of "*kosher*" appliances that come with a Shabbat mode. This involves a time delay from when a switch is touched to when the appliance comes on. That time delay, referred to as a *gramma* or indirect action, makes it okay to turn on these specially-rigged appliances so that food can be heated up. It is also permissible to turn on an electric or gas stove before the Sabbath, and leave it on until the end of Shabbat.
- No laundry can be done on the Sabbath including the washing or bleaching of a garment in any manner, no wringing out a wet garment, and spots or stains cannot be removed from clothing.
- No sewing or needlework is allowed, nor any taping, pasting, or stapling.
- No building or assembling of items (puzzles, etc.)

The Messiah and the World To Come (Heaven)

The Messiah

Belief in the eventual coming of the *Messiah* is a basic and fundamental part of traditional Judaism. The Messiah (derived from the Hebrew, meaning, "the anointed one") will be recognized by Jews and non-Jews alike and he will teach the world how to live by God's Torah. Life will be easy and we will no longer have to work for a living. Women will give birth quickly and easily, without difficult pregnancies and without painful labor and childbirth. Life spans will be very prolonged, disease will no longer exist, and pain will be eradicated. Eventually all sin will disappear completely.

Hard Core Jewish People believe that in each generation, there is at least one righteous person who is worthy of being the Messiah. This will come to fruition if the generation repents and the time is right for the Messiah to come. [I tell Barry that we'd better be nice to Carter, because he might be the Messiah.] The Messiah will bring peace and affluence to the world so that everyone will be able to peacefully pursue their purpose in life — to serve *Hashem* through *Torah* study and prayer. [But what if I don't want that to be my purpose in life? Oh well!] The job of the *Jewish Nation* is to repent and perform good deeds in order to hasten the Messiah's arrival. The Jewish Nation is considered one unit. Therefore the actions of one person can change the fate of the entire group. Says the *Talmud* (Oral Torah, Yoma 86b), "If one person does a sincere *teshuva* (return to God), then the whole world merits forgiveness." [Hey Carter, we're counting on you!]

In the modern period, Jews have reexamined the traditional notion of the Messiah. While some Jews continue to hope and pray for a personal Messiah, many believe in the coming of a Messianic Age, a time of peace and prosperity for all people on earth, fulfilling God's plan for humanity. For some, it is a fervent belief in a time that will come to pass; for others, the Messianic Age represents a goal toward which they orient their lives and hopes, for it informs them how to live their lives. Their prayers are oriented toward the Messianic Age, the coming of a time of peace and tranquility, with the full expectation that their prayers and actions will be consistent, day in and day out.

The fundamental difference between Judaism and Christianity is that Christians believe that Christ was the Messiah, while Jews are still awaiting their Messiah. Jews do not believe that Jesus was the Messiah because he did not uphold the two primary elements of the Messiah and the Messianic Age: justice and peace. This point was made crystal clear by his own gruesome death. Christianity acknowledges this by stating that there will be a "second coming" of the Messiah.

The World To Come

Judaism divides Jews' existence in the universe into two time periods: This World (*Olam Hazeh*) and the World To Come (WTC; *Olam Habah* or the Jewish version of heaven). Man earns his reward in This World by fulfilling *mitzvot* (commandments) while the World To Come is the ultimate reward — the closest possible connection to God. It is frequently explained and emphasized in the Talmud that life on this earth is only a preparation for the future and everlasting life in the World To Come. To religious Jews, death is simply a transition from one life into another. Essentially, there is no afterlife. Rather, the soul survives death and is liberated from the body. The Jewish People believe that human suffering is nothing in comparison to the glory of God's love in the afterlife. [You have to remember that the Jewish People don't mind delayed gratification.]

While Hard Core Jewish People perform mitzvot out of a sense of love of God and a sacred obligation to do so, they are also looking forward to a big "share" in the WTC. The mainstream Jewish view, clearly expressed in the Bible and rabbinic literature, is that God will reward those who observe His commandments and punish those who intentionally transgress them. I'd say the operative word here is "intentionally." To me that means that if I am ignorant of Torah law, then I don't get blamed by God for my violations. Of course, Carter has a rebuttal for that line of thinking. [Is it just me, or are there others who think that up to now, everyone must have misinterpreted the Torah? Please tell me that God did not intend for mankind to keep Him top-of-mind at all times – there's so many other things going on in this incredible world.]

While many good deeds have rewards in This World that can be appreciated and enjoyed during this lifetime, the primary results and effects of good deeds will be manifest in the World To Come. The more commandments one performs, the higher their elevation or stance in the World To Come. A particularly righteous person will have a greater share than the average person. Also, a person can lose his/her share through wicked actions. The good news for me is that Judaism recognizes that it is mankind's nature to rebel against authority. Thus, one who does something because he is commanded to is regarded with greater merit than one who does something because he chooses to. Hot damn! When I light the *Sabbath* candles, I rarely feel like doing it so I get more credit than I would if it was something I enjoyed because it takes more effort to make myself do it. . Those of us on the dark side who are into success, materialism, romantic love, and hedonism are content to live more leisurely and spontaneously here on Earth and settle for less of a share in life after death. I'll take my chances because our souls can be elevated after we die by our loved ones saying *kaddish* (prayers) for us or by making donations to Jewish causes. I like being able to delegate my soul elevation to the kaddish brigade and live life to the fullest now.

According to Rabbi Shraga Simmons at Aish.com, people like me are being short-sighted. "When a person dies and goes to heaven, the judgment is not arbitrary and externally imposed. Rather, the soul is shown two videotapes. The first video is called 'This is Your Life!' Every decision and every thought, all the good deeds, and the embarrassing things a person did in private are all replayed without any embellishments. It's fully bared for all to see."

"The second video depicts how a person's life "could have been...if the right choices had been made, if the opportunities were seized, if the potential was actualized. This video - the pain of squandered potential — is much more difficult to bear. But at the same time it purifies the soul as well. The pain creates regret which removes the barriers and enables the soul to completely connect to God."

The thing is that very little is known about the World To Come and I may not like it. The *Talmud* (Oral Torah) says that even the *Prophets* could not see more than dimly into the World To Come. Only Hashem knows clearly the details of it. The Talmud describes Shabbat as a taste of the World To Come. When God gave Israel the Torah, He promised that if the people would keep His commandments, they would be rewarded in the World To Come. The Israelites hadn't the slightest idea what God was promising, so God gave them Shabbat as a sample. What is known about the WTC is that there will be no eating or drinking, nor any other physical needs. The whole world will recognize the Jewish God as the only true God and the Jewish religion as the only true religion. There will be no murder, robbery, competition or jealousy. There will be no sin. But having no physical pleasures doesn't sound like a fun time to me.

Death and Mourning Rituals

Death Rituals

Judaism accepts and encourages the expression of deep grief following the death of a loved one. It encourages tears; it accepts that death is sometimes tragic for the mourners and it does not make false attempts to comfort at a time of deep grief. It accepts that death can be so tragic that people are sometimes unable to cope with life at that moment, calling forth the need for care by the community. But this grief, having been allowed to express itself, must find its own limits; endless grieving amidst personal self-neglect, cut off from community support, is not the way of Judaism. Grief for those who have died is balanced by the needs of those left living. The irrationality and essential passionate wildness of raw pain, must, over time, be placed in overall proportion.

After a person dies, there is an entire procedure of cleansing and preparing the body, with customs varying from community to community. The eyes are closed, the body is laid on the floor and covered, and candles are lit next to the body. The body is never left alone until after burial as a sign of respect. The people who sit with the dead body are called *shomerim*, meaning "guards" or "keepers." Respect for the dead body is a matter of paramount importance. The shomerim may not eat, drink, or perform a commandment in the presence of the dead. To do so would be considered mocking the dead, because the dead can no longer do these things.

Jewish tradition encourages a very quick burial. If possible, the burial should take place on the same day as the death. It is considered disrespectful toward the dead to delay the burial any more than in absolutely necessary. However, if time is needed for some of the close family to get to the place where the dead is being buried, the burial can be delayed. It is considered potentially dishonorable to the dead person to prevent their being buried without all of their loved ones present.

The body is never displayed at funerals; open casket ceremonies are forbidden by Jewish law. According to Jewish law, exposing a body is considered disrespectful because it allows not only friends, but also enemies to view the dead, mocking their helpless state. Autopsies in general are discouraged as desecration of the body. They are considered the highest form of insult to the deceased and can only be performed under suspicion of foul play, and even then only after consultation with a competent Orthodox rabbi. When autopsies must be performed, they should be minimally intrusive.

In preparation for the burial, the body is thoroughly cleaned and wrapped in a simple, plain white linen shroud. Only Torah-true Jews may touch the body of an Observant Jew. The Sages decreed that both the dress of the body and the coffin should be simple, so that a poor person would not receive less honor in death than a rich person. The body is not embalmed, and no organs or fluids may be removed. All body fluids are considered part of the body and are to be buried with it. Regarding organ donation, according to some sources it is permitted because the subsequent burial of the recipient will satisfy the requirement of burying the entire original body. The body must not be cremated. It must be buried in the earth. Coffins are not required but if they are used, they must have holes drilled in them so the body comes in contact with the earth.

Mourning Rituals (or Sitting Shiva)

In the Jewish tradition, *shiva* is the seven-day mourning period that begins immediately after the funeral of a parent, spouse, child, or a brother or sister. The purpose of shiva is to bring people together immediately following a funeral to remember the departed, and in remembering, celebrate the life once lived. It is an opportunity to honor the loved one's death and to help comprehend and accept it. The custom stems directly from the verse in Genesis in which Joseph mourns his father, Jacob, for a week. During the seven days, Jewish mourning rituals are extensive and ensure that mourners will remain catatonic and depressed. Family members are to suspend all worldly activities and devote full attention to remembering and mourning the deceased. Mourners sit on low stools or the floor instead of chairs, do not wear leather shoes, do not shave or cut their hair, do not wear cosmetics, do not work, and do not do things for comfort or pleasure, such as bathe for pleasure, have sex, put on fresh clothing, or study *Torah* (except Torah related to mourning and grief). Mourners wear the clothes that they tore at the time of learning of the death or at the funeral. Mirrors in the house are covered because it is believed that by discarding vanity and being unkempt, inner reflection as to the meaning of life and death will be encouraged. [Whatever!] Prayer services are held with friends, neighbors and relatives making up the *minyan* (10 people required for certain prayers).

Immediately after the funeral, those who go to visit the mourners while they are sitting shiva are required to wash their hands before entering the home. This is done because a dead body is considered a source of ritual impurity and the water symbolically removes any contamination. The mourners typically leave a basin outside the front door along with a towel for this purpose.

After Shiva

For a year following a loved one's death, Hard Cores say *kaddish* for that person on a daily basis, or they hire someone to say it. Jewish law specifies that the souls of the departed can be elevated in heaven by the deeds and prayers of the living — especially descendents of the living or Torah students. [I'm going to look to Carter to say kaddish for me after I kick-the-bucket so I can be elevated in the World To Come and keep rocking-out in this world.]

Jewish law requires that a tombstone be prepared so that the deceased will not be forgotten and the grave will not be desecrated. It is customary in some communities to keep the tombstone veiled, or to delay putting it up until the end of the 12-month mourning period. The idea underlying this custom is that the dead will not be forgotten when he/she is being mourned every day. In communities where this custom is observed, there is generally a formal unveiling ceremony when the tombstone is revealed.

It is also customary in some communities to place small stones on a gravesite when visiting it. The custom is not universal, even among traditional Jews, and there is some doubt as to how it originated. It seems to have superstitious origins. It's a little like leaving a calling card for the dead person, to let them know you were there. Stones, unlike flowers, are permanent and do not get blown away in the wind.

SECTION III: GLOSSARY

A Jewish Dictionary

Please note that most of the words in this glossary are transliterated from Hebrew. As such, there may be a variety of different ways to spell and/or pronounce them in English. If you've noticed that Hanukkah can also be correctly spelled as Chanukah, then you've experienced this transliteration phenomenon. Dig it.

Abraham (like Lincoln) - Abraham is widely considered to be the father of mono-theism – the first person to deny the existence of multiple gods (e.g., the god of fire, god of wind, etc.) and say that there is only one God. Ironically, he was the son of an idol-maker and was born in what is now Iraq.

Aliyah (ol-ee-YAH) - The process of moving to Israel to become an Israeli citizen.

Ashkenazi (osh-ken-AZ-ee) - One of two sects of Judaism, the other being Sephardi. Ashkenazi Jews were originally from Europe and spoke Yiddish, while Sephardi Jews were originally from Middle Eastern or Spanish countries and spoke Ladino.

Aufruf (OOF-roof) - This is a tradition where the groom goes to the synagogue on the Sabbath prior to the wedding in order to announce his plans to marry to the congregation while also playing an active role in the service. Those in the audience typically throw candy at the groom, symbolizing their wishes for a sweet life.

Baruch Hashem (bah-ROOK HA-shem) - "Blessed God." A casual phrase, like "Thank God" in English.

Ba'al Teshuva (BAHL CHEW-vuh) - Literally, "One Who Owns Redemption." Refers to people who were not raised as Observant Jews but became observant, or people who were raised observant, turned away, and then returned.

Bedeken (buh-DECK-in) - This is the ceremony that takes place immediately before the wedding in which the groom covers the brides face with her veil.

Beshert (buh-SHAIRT) - Willed by God or meant to be.

Bitul (bih-TOOL) - This is a *Hassidic* concept that true happiness comes not from what one does, but by focusing on what has been given to him or her in life.

Bris (rhymes with kiss) - Religious circumcision

Chassan (HA-sahn) - Groom

Chazal (ha-ZAHL) - Sages

Chessed (HEH-sid) - Jewish virtues

Chosen People - Jews are called the Chosen People because they were selected to serve God and thus to serve mankind by spreading the notion of one God to the world along with a system of ethics and morals.

Chametz (HUM-metz) - Foods comprised of certain ingredients such as grains that are forbidden to be in one's home during Passover.

Chuppah (HOOP-puh) - A flower-covered canopy under which the wedding ceremony is conducted.

Chutzpah (HOOTS-puh) - Yiddish word for guts or audacity.

Daven (DAH-vin) - Verb meaning "to pray."

Emunah (ee-MOO-nuh) - Faith in God.

Eruv (EE-roove) - This is defined in Judaic religious law as an area where Observant Jews are freed from the Sabbath prohibition of carrying items. For Observant Jews, a home within the eruv can greatly improve the quality of life because there they are allowed to push a baby carriage, carry food to friends' homes, or tote a diaper bag. Outside the eruv on the Sabbath, Jews are not allowed to do these things.

Fleyshik (FLY-shick) - This refers to Meat and includes the kosher meat or bones of mammals and fowl, soups or gravies made with them, and any food containing even a small quantity of the above. Kosher laws prohibit Meat and Dairy from being combined or eaten at the same time. There is no explanation as to the reason for this in the Torah other than God told the Jewish People to do so. Separate utensils are used for each, and a waiting period is observed between eating them if meat is eaten first.

Frum (FROOM) - Religious. To say "I am a *frum* Jew" means "I am a very religious Jew." *Frum* is a term usually only used nowadays to refer to Orthodox or Ultra-Orthodox Jews.

Frum-From-Birth (FFB) - Someone who was raised as an Orthodox Jew, as opposed to someone who became religious at some later point in their life.

G-d - The way of writing the name of the divine such that if the document is discarded, Hashem's name is not destroyed.

Gemara (guh-MORE-uh) - The second half of the Talmud which contains commentary on the Mishnah. The other half is the Mishnah - the Gemara is in fact commentary on the Mishnah, which is commentary on the Torah, and the Mishnah and the Gemara make up the Talmud (*See also "Talmud"*).

Get - The official proclamation of divorce for Orthodox Jews.

Gezeirah (See also "Rabbinic Law") - A rule instituted by the rabbis to prevent inadvertent violation of a mitzvah. For instance, it is a mitzvah to refrain from work on the Sabbath, but a gezeirah to avoid even the handling of any work implements on the Sabbath.

Gramma (GRAM-muh) - This refers to the concept of a time-delay between one's actions (like turning on a switch) and the reaction (electrification of a heating element) to enable otherwise forbidden actions to be done on the Sabbath. Modern technology built into ovens and other appliances applies this concept so they can be used without breaking such laws.

Ha-Kadosh Boruch Hu - Literally, "The Holy One, Blessed Be He." Another name of God, one which can be written because it is not actually a proper name.

Halacha (huh-LOCK-ah) - "Law" - Jewish law, whether Torah law (laws given to us in the Torah by God) or Rabbinical law. Halacha includes codes of behavior, applicable to virtually every imaginable circumstance, (and many hypothetical ones) which have been pored over and developed through the generations. Halacha governs not just religious life, but daily life as well including how to dress, what to eat, and how to help the poor. Observance of Halacha shows gratitude to God, provides a sense of Jewish identity, and brings the sacred into everyday life. A traditional Jewish question is not "What do you believe?" but rather, "What is the *halacha* (law)?" This is because Judaism, a product of the Eastern World, emphasizes "correct behavior" over "correct thinking".

Haredi (ha-REED-ee) - The term means "God-fearing" or one who trembles in awe of God. Also referred to as ultra-Orthodox Jews, they consider their belief system and religious practices to extend in an unbroken chain back to Moses and the giving of the Torah on Mt. Sinai. As a result, they consider non-Orthodox denominations to be unjustifiable deviations from authentic Judaism. *Haredim* (ha-REED-dim) is the plural.

Hashem (ha-SHEM) - The lowest name of God, in that it is not even a proper name - literally, it means "The Name" in Hebrew. It can be spoken of lightly and written without concern.

Hassid (HA-sid) - This is a person of piety, even higher than a *tzaddik*, in that he conducts himself beyond the letter of the law. This is the root of the word Hassidic. Also spelled Chassid.

Heksher (HECK-sure) - Symbol of kashrut supervision (level of kosherness) on packaged foods. Since even a small trace of a non-kosher substance can render a food not kosher, all processed foods and eating establishments require certification by a reliable rabbi or kashrut supervising agency. The OU (actually a U within a circle) and Star K symbols are the most common certification symbols seen on kosher foods.

Jewish Values - Judaism matters to the whole world because it is a system for making human beings decent. Jewish values include: Being good, Being kind, Being ethical, and Being moral. Jews are supposed to serve as an example for the rest of the world.

Kabbalah (kuh-BAHL-uh) - Kabbalah is a branch of Jewish mysticism whose goal is to uncover the reality hidden under layers of what we in this world perceive to be reality. We live in a world of appearances and perceptions which mask the underlying reality of all beings and all Creation. Kabbalah (meaning "that which has been received") is the intellectual and methodological approach to accessing the timeless truth of reality in the here and now. In other words, it is the process of acquiring and practicing esoteric knowledge and techniques for glimpsing the reality beyond our material world — ultimately, for "glimpsing" the Ultimate Reality, God. Academics would term this "communing with the godhead." In this regard, most mystical religious practices share a common search for the underlying reality that grounds all being; Jewish Kabbalah promotes additional goals deriving from Jewish values, and its own particular methods and practices related to Jewish sacred texts and traditions. Like all mystical practices, it is rich in metaphor and employs a vocabulary which invests "old words" with new meaning.

Kaddish (COD-ish) - Kaddish is a traditional prayer said by mourners for the dead and also said as part of the synagogue prayer service; it does not mention death but rather serves as an affirmation of God's existence.

Kallah (KOLL-lah) - Bride

*Kashrut (*KOSH-root; *See also "Kosher")* - These are the Torah commandments and rabbinic laws that have no explanation but which are obediently and diligently followed by Orthodox Jews. Kashrut includes exactly which foods may and may not be eaten, how food must be prepared (e.g., meat and dairy may not be eaten in the same meal; animals must be humanely killed in a prescribed manner; fish without fins or scales, shellfish, and pork may not be eaten). Something that Hard Core Jewish People can eat is kosher; something that Hard Core Jewish People cannot eat is unkosher or *traif.*

Kedushah (keh-DOO-shuh) - Holiness.

Ketubah (kuh-TOO-buh) - This is the official marriage contract between bride and groom signed by the groom and officiating rabbi as well as the fathers. It details the husband's obligations to the wife, including food, shelter, and sexual relations.

Kiddushin (kih-DOO-shin) - The first part of the wedding ceremony, it is the betrothal ceremony bonding two souls with each other and with God.

Kippa (KEEP-uh) - A skull cap, yarmulke, or head covering worn by Orthodox men, but not required of women.

Kiruv (KEY-roove) - Jewish outreach, or the attempt to save the souls of unaffiliated and moderately-affiliated Jews with the goal of bringing them closer to their Jewish heritage.

Kittel (rhymes with little) - A long white bathrobe-type gown traditionally worn over the groom's clothing during an Orthodox wedding.

Kosher - Kosher or *kashrut* laws define the foods that are fit for the consumption of a Jew. Keeping kosher is a *mitzvah*, a divine commandment and connection. The Jewish People eat kosher because God commanded them to, and by fulfilling this commandment they connect to God.

Kotel (rhymes with hotel) - The Kotel is part of the western supporting wall of the Temple Mount and is the only remains of the second temple. It has become the most hallowed spot in Jewish religious and national consciousness and tradition. Also known as the Wailing Wall and Western Wall.

Loshon Hora (luh-SHON HO-rah) - This refers to the *halachic* prohibitions against gossip and what you can and cannot say about others.

Maimonides (pronounced my-MON-i-dees) - Moses Maimonides (1135-1204), also known as the "Rambam," was a medieval Jewish rabbi, physician, and philosopher and one of the most influential post-Talmudic scholars. His major contribution to Jewish life was the Mishneh Torah, his code of Jewish law. Rambam's intention was to compose a book that would guide Jews on how to behave in all situations just by reading the Torah and his code, without having to expend large amounts of time searching through the Talmud. Carter and his mentors at Aish HaTorah regard Rambam's Code as authoritative.

Mechitzah (meh-HEATS-uh) - The term used for the designated areas of a synagogue that create sacred spaces for each gender to connect with Hashem without distraction.

Melachah (mel-AH-ha) - This is the type of work forbidden on the Sabbath. It is defined as work that is creative or exerts control over one's environment.

The Messiah - The Messiah will be the first king during the Messianic Era. He will bring peace to the world and show Jews the proper understanding of how to serve Hashem and to fulfill themselves spiritually. Hard Core Jewish People believe that by living the life prescribed by God, a person can actually hasten the coming of the messiah.

Messianic Age - The start of the Messianic Age will be the Time of Redemption. The world will begin to better itself spiritually. The physical nature of the world will not change, but life spans will be very prolonged. Disease will disappear entirely, pain will be eradicated, and all the curses Adam and Eve received for their sin of eating the apple will be nullified. Women will give birth quickly and easily, without difficult pregnancies and without painful labor and childbirth. Life will be easy and we will no longer have to work for a living.

Loaves of bread will grow on trees, and clothing will be readily available. There will be no oppression, no war, and no crime anywhere on earth. All sin will disappear completely. Our main function will be the attainment of spiritual growth.

Metzitzah b'peh (meh-TSITS-uh BUH-peh) - This is the custom of the *mohel* using his mouth to suck the blood from the penis of the baby boy immediately following the removal of the foreskin during the *bris* (religious circumcision).

Mezuzah (meh-ZUZ-ah) - The ornament (approximately 3-4" long and less than an inch wide attached to the doorframe of the front door of one's home (as well as rooms within the home) in accordance with the *Shema* and Jewish law. It houses a handwritten scroll containing the words of the Shema (though inexpensive versions are machine-printed). It is placed on the right frame of the door (looking in) at about eye-level and slants slightly inward.

Midrash (MID-rosh) - Comprises multiple interpretations proffered by mortals of God's intended meaning of everything in the Torah. Sometimes the interpretations contradict each other. *(See also "Talmud")*

Mikveh (MICK-vuh) - This is a body of water used solely for ritual purification — not physical cleanliness. It is primarily used by women at the conclusion of their menstrual period in order to purify themselves so they can be touched by their husband. Observant men sometimes immerse themselves in the mikveh before the Sabbath or a holiday and it is also used by post-menstruating women and converts to Judaism. One must thoroughly bathe before entering a mikveh. This body of water must contain at least 480 liters of water that has not been drawn or stored in a vessel. Oceans, lakes, rivers, ponds and springs are all natural catch basins of rainwater, and thus can be used as mikvot (plural for mikveh).

Milkhik (MIL-kick) - This refers to Dairy and includes the milk of any kosher animal, all milk products made with it (e.g., cream, butter, cheese, etc.), and any food containing even a small quantity of the above. Kosher laws prohibit Meat and Dairy from being combined or eaten at the same time. There is no explanation as to the reason for this in the Torah other than God told the Jewish People to do it. Separate utensils are used for each, and a waiting period is observed between eating them if meat is eaten first.

Minhag (MIN-hog) - A custom that evolved for worthy religious reasons and that has continued long enough to become a binding religious practice. While customs are usually more recent inventions and can vary from place to place, there is a Jewish law saying that you should observe the customs of your community as if they were laws, which effectively makes them as binding as any Jewish law. An example of a Minhag is on the holiday of Shavuos, Observant Jews stay up all night in the synagogue and study to show God how much they love the Torah. Another example is the observance of Passover for an additional day everywhere except in Israel. A Minhag also refers to an act inspired by regional perspective and culture, such as standing in synagogue when the Ten Commandments are read. *(See also "Rabbinic Law")*

Minyan (MIN-yun) - A quorum of ten Jewish adult males (ages 13 and older) needed to say certain prayers.

Mishnah (MISH-nuh) - The first half of the Talmud and contains commentary on the Torah. *(See also "Talmud")*

Mitzvah (MITZ-vuh) - The word "mitzvah" means "commandment" or "obligation." The plural for the word is *mitzvot.*

Modern Orthodox Jews - Unlike Orthodox Jews who strictly follow Torah law, Modern Orthodox Jews value traditional Jewish life but are willing to deviate from halachically-required Jewish practices when they believe it to be personally necessary or appropriate to do so.

Mohel (MOIL, rhymes with boil) - The Mohel is a person of the Jewish faith who is ordained to do circumcision under the guidelines of the Jewish religion. Mohelim (plural) receive certification and medical training in circumcision as well as training on how to do the procedure within the specifications of the Jewish religion.

Moschiach (moe-SHEE-ah) - The Messiah.

Niddah (KNEE-duh) - The state of menstruating. It is considered a ritually impure state when sexual intercourse (or even touching your husband) is prohibited.

Nisuin (nih-SOO-in) - The second part of the wedding ceremony, which provides spiritual elevation for the couple as several participants (including rabbis) honor them with blessings.

Olam Habah (OWE-lem hah-BAH) - The World To Come, or the Jewish version of heaven. It is a time rather than a place. It will involve a rebirth of the physical world and will be a world of light, of only happiness and delight; a time of closeness to Hashem and of understanding His ways; a blissful time of knowing and experiencing the truth and basking in everlasting joy and peace in a world that is entirely *Shabbat*. Longing and hoping for that time opens one's eyes to observe and appreciate the goodness and loving-kindness that Hashem showers upon us. It enriches one's life with true contentment and peace.

Olam Hazeh (OWE-lem hah-ZAY) – This is the world of here and now. Jews are to regard all challenges in this world as preparation for the World To Come.

Onah (rhymes with the whale guy, Jonah) - Onah is the right of a woman to expect to have sexual intercourse with her husband. It is one of the five basic rights of a woman – the others being food, clothing, shelter, and emotional understanding.

Pareve (PARVE) - Something that is neither meat nor dairy, and can be eaten with either without breaking kosher law. A *pareve* cake can be eaten directly after a meat or dairy meal, while a dairy cake cannot.

Prophets - Prophets are humans who have raised themselves to a high level. Moses was the greatest of all prophets. Prophecy comes to a righteous person who has greatly developed his character in service of Hashem.

Rabbinic Law - In addition to the 613 mitzvot, Jewish law incorporates a large body of rabbinical rules and laws. These are considered just as binding as the mitzvot, although the punishments for violating them are less severe. Rabbinic law falls into three groups: a Gezeirah, Takkanah, and Minhag.

> *Gezeirah* - a rule instituted by the rabbis to prevent inadvertent violation of a mitzvah. For instance, it is a mitzvah to refrain from work on the Sabbath, but a gezeirah to avoid even the handling of any work implements on the Sabbath.

> Takkanah - a law instituted by rabbis that does not derive from the Torah. For example, the lighting of candles on Chanukah and the banning of polygamy.

> *Minhag* - a custom that evolved for worthy religious reasons and that has continued long enough to become a binding religious practice. For example, on the holiday of Shavuos, Observant Jews stay up all night in the

synagogue and study to show God how much they love the Torah. Another example is the observance of Passover for an additional day everywhere except in Israel. A Minhag also refers to an act inspired by regional perspective and culture, such as standing in synagogue when the Ten Commandments are read.

Rachmanus (rock-MOAN-us) - This comprises compassion, love, and concern, the greatest virtues of the Jews.

Rebbetzin (REB-bets-in) - A rabbi's wife. This term can also refer to a married female teacher, even if she is not a rabbi's wife.

Ruach (ROO-ah) - Spirit. To "*daven* with a lot of *ruach*" means to pray with a lot of spirit or intention.

Sanhedrin (san-HEAD-drin) - Ancient Jewish Parliament

Seder (SAY-der) - The session combining prayers, wine, food, and singing that takes place on the first two nights of Passover. This event can last well into the night and often doesn't end until the wee hours.

Smicha (SMEEK-ha) - This is a rabbinic ordination document given to those who have gone through a rigorous course of Jewish study and testing. The document confirms that the individual has the authority to judge Jewish law and he should be called a rabbi and relied upon to have halachic authority. Orthodoxy only allows men to receive this honor.

Traditionally, rabbinic ordination is not given by an institution or by a yeshiva. Rather, it is given directly by a student's individual Rabbi who taught and tested him. The quality or prestige of a Smicha is directly related to the level of Torah scholarship and Torah expertise achieved by one's teacher who awards the Smicha. Ordination usually requires completion of a college degree followed by a 4- or 5-year program at a Jewish seminary with an additional preparatory year required for students without sufficient grounding in Hebrew and Jewish studies [like Carter].

Sephardi (suh-FAR-dee) - One of two sects of Judaism, the other being Ashkenazi. Sephardi Jews were originally from the Middle Eastern or Spanish countries and spoke Ladino. Plural: Sephardim

Shabbat (or Shabbas, or Sabbath) - The proper Hebrew term is Shabbot, but Ashkenazi Jews refer to it as Shabbos. The Sabbath begins on Friday at 18 minutes before sundown and ends Saturday night when three stars appear in the sky. During this 25-hour period is an intense spiritual retreat in which the religious Jew adheres to special laws meant to increase the holiness of the day.

Shabbos Goy - A non-Jew you get to do things for you on *Shabbos*, such as turn on lights and cover for you at work. Non-Jews are not part of Abraham's Covenant and therefore are not required to perform the commandments of the Torah, but also do not receive the benefits of the commandments. It is well known in Jewish circles that Elvis was a *Shabbos Goy* at one point in his life.

Sh'chatat zerah (shuh-HOT-tot ZEE-rah) - Destruction of human seed (sperm), defined as ejaculation outside the vagina.

Sheggitz (SHEG-its) - Derogatory term for a non-Jewish man.

Sheitel (also Sheidel; rhymes with cradle) - A wig, worn by a married woman, who is not permitted to show her hair (according to Orthodox Judaism). While a normal head covering will suffice, the sheitel is often just more aesthetically appeasing and so is preferred.

Shema (shuh-MA) - The single most important prayer in Judaism, outlining the basic actions advised by God.

Shidduch (SHIH-duke) - A match or a marriage. Also a meeting.

Shiksah (SHICK-suh) - A derogatory term for a female non-Jewish person.

Shiva (SHIV-uh) - People "sit shiva" following someone's death. The custom typically takes place at the home of the family of the deceased during a seven-day period of mourning. Prayers are said for the deceased and food is served to those who visit.

Shmatte (SHMOT-tuh) - Yiddish for a ragged piece of clothing.

Shomer Negiah (SHOW-mare nuh-GIE-uh) - "To Guard the Touch" - to not touch members of the opposite sex, except for your spouse, members of your immediate family, or in a medical emergency.

Shomer Shabbos - Literally: "To Guard the Sabbath;" this refers to someone who observes the laws of Shabbat

Shomerim (show-mare-REEM) - These are the people who sit with a dead body to "guard" it prior to burial.

Shul (rhymes with pool) - Refers to the synagogue and surrounding structures if related to religious activities.

Simchah (SIM-kah) - A Jewish festive occasion is called a simchah, which is the Hebrew word for "joy."

Spirituality - A sense of connection to the universe and to a higher power.

Sukkah (SOOK-ah) – This is a three-sided temporary shelter, usually with a roof made of branches from a tree, used during the celebration of Sukkot.

Sukkot (SUE-coat) - One of the key holidays of the Jewish year, celebrated for eight days during late-September or

October, it commemorates the 40 years of wandering in the desert after the flight out of Egypt.

Taharah (tuh-HAR-uh) - Purity.

Takkanah (tah-KAN-nuh) - A law instituted by rabbis that is not derived from the Torah. For example, the lighting of candles on Chanukah and the banning of polygamy. *(See also "Rabbinic Law")*

Tallit (TOLL-it) - The prayer shawl worn by men during services, this garment is generally white with fringe and is intended to remind one of his obligations to God.

Talmud (TAHL-muhd) - This is the Oral Torah that contains a collection of rabbinical commentaries and rulings that provide interpretation and application of the Laws. The first half of the Talmud is the Mishnah, a commentary on the Torah, and the second half is the Gemara, a commentary on the Mishnah.

Tanakh (tuh-KNOCK) - The written Torah.

Tefillin (tuh-FILL-in) - Prayer boxes which men must wear once a day except on *Shabbat* and holidays, according to the laws of the Torah.

Tehillim (teh-HEEL-em) - The psalms written by *David Ha-Melech* (King David). Reciting *tehillim* is kind of an Orthodox pastime, and a way of asking God for things, usually healing or to find a husband. It is common in Orthodox circles to hear the phrase "I'm saying *tehillim* for so-and-so, who is sick."

The Temple - The Temple refers to the place in Jerusalem that was the center of Jewish religion from the time of Solomon to its destruction by the Romans in 70 C.E. This was the one and only place where sacrifices and certain other religious rituals were performed. It was partially destroyed at the time of the Babylonian exile and rebuilt. The rebuilt temple was known as the Second Temple. The famous Wailing Wall is the western retaining wall of that Temple, and is as close to the site of the original Sanctuary as Jews can go today. The site of The Temple is currently occupied by a Moslem Mosque, the Dome of the Rock.

Teshuva (tuh-SHOO-vuh) - Being sorry for having disobeyed God and remedying the error by becoming a servant of God. One does *teshuva* to compensate for a bad deed.

Tikkun Olam (tih-KOON OH-lum) - Repair of the world through the pursuit of social justice, considered to be a central precept of Judaism.

Toivel (TOY-vull) - The process of immersing household items involved in the cooking process in a *mikveh* in order to render them acceptable for use in the preparation of kosher meals. Also, the placement of cookware in boiling water to purify them for use during Passover.

Torah - The Torah is a religious book that describes the way the Jewish tradition views their relationship to God, God's relationship to them, and their mutual obligations to God and to each other. By Torah, it also includes everything that the rabbis have taught in concert with the Torah, because that is part of the original Torah.

Traif (TRAYF) - Something that is not kosher and therefore cannot be eaten by a kosher Jew.

Tsneis (SNEE-is) - Modesty. The modesty laws for women are: One must always wear a skirt that extends to an inch below the knee. One must always wear a shirt that has sleeves that reach the elbows, and a high collar that does not show the collar bone. Married women must cover their hair. Some communities ask that women also wear black stockings. The male modesty laws are much less strict and vary from community to community.

Tzaddik (SOD-dick) - Literally, one who is righteous; a tzaddik is one who acquires the highest level of righteousness – the Jewish "saint." *(See also "Hassid")*

*Tzitzit (*TSIT-see) - The knotted strings that must be attached to every four-cornered male garment, as commanded by God in Leviticus. The knots add up to 613, the number of commandments in the Torah. You will sometimes see the strings hanging outside a man's pants.

Vort - The traditional "engagement party" at which the groom is praised by the guests.

Written Torah - This comprises the Old Testament (The Five Books of Moses) and is also known as *Tanakh*.

Yahrzeit (YART-sight) - Anniversary of a death as calculated on the Hebrew calendar.

Yeshiva (yuh-SHE-vah) - A school of Jewish learning. The plural is yeshivot.

Yeshiva Bochur (yuh-SHE-vah bah-HOOR) - An unmarried male, who largely sits in yeshiva and studies to keep himself busy before he gets married, in the Orthodox scheme of things.

Yetzah Hora (YETS-uh HOAR-uh) - The evil inclination - much like the Christian devil, who tempts, but it is not a single force but many small inclinations.

Yichud (YICK-hod) - The room to which the bride and groom go immediately following the wedding ceremony to spend a few minutes together alone.

Yiddishkeit (YID-dish-kite) - Yiddish, meaning "Jewishness;" a word similar to Orthodoxy and Observance, but suggesting more of an emotional attachment and a feeling of identification with the Jewish People rather than a full commitment to a lifestyle based on observance of the 613 commandments of God, as recorded in the Torah.

Yoledet (yoe-luh-DET) - A time of female ritual impurity that begins in the later stages of labor as defined by a woman's inability to walk without assistance and extends until after the birth of the child, the length of which is determined by the gender of the baby. During this time, her husband may not touch her and must treat her in the same manner as when she is *niddah*.

ACKNOWLEDGEMENTS

I am greatly indebted to:

My son Carter, whose brave search to discover that missing piece in life led him into the world of the Hard Core Jewish People and served as the inspiration for my expanded knowledge of God, Jews, and spirituality – and, of course, was the impetus for this book.

My husband, Barry, for his patience in letting me bounce ideas off of him, for listening to me pontificate about this book for nearly a year, and for his assistance in grammatical, historical, and spelling editing.

My son Tyler Blue, my brother Philip, Bonna, Ted, Lois, and Hilarie, who read chapters and gave me feedback so I'd know if the book was at all boring.

Carol and Stuart, Carter's in-laws, for their ongoing support. Margie and Mitch, and all of our friends and relatives for the encouragement they proffered along the way.

Naomi, my wonderful daughter-in-law, Carter, and my cousin Aaron (who we refer to as Moses) who helped check the book for Jewish accuracy while enduring the irreverence which sometimes pained them in that they are Torah-true Jews. However, they consistently urged me on and understood from the beginning how important it is that the sassy tone be used to reflect my personality and get people to read the book who don't even think they have an interest in Judaism.

David, Larry, Jared, Lauren, and all of Carter's friends who encouraged me along the way and added fuel to my fire.

Azriela Jaffe, an author of 13 published books and a righteous Jewish woman, who so kindly emailed a synopsis of my book to her editor, Altie Karper, Managing Editor of Schocken Books, the Jewish division of Random House.

Altie Karper, who took the time to read my synopsis and five chapters of the book two months after I had started writing it. She told me that "this is an interesting idea for a book" and gave me suggestions as to what direction I should go in. From that point on, I moved full-speed ahead.

BIBLIOGRAPHY

Listed below are Internet sites that I consulted while doing research for this book. This list will come in handy for readers who want to further pursue the topic, and those who want to check out my sources for accuracy.

http://
en.wikipedia.org
Judaism.about.com
jewish.com
judaism.about.com
ohr.edu
shma.com
shamash.org

http://www.
aish.com
answers.com
beingjewish.com
beliefnet.com
chabad.org
chayas.com
chosen-people.com
darchenoam.org
everythingjewish.com
faqs.org
forward.com
hanefesh.com
heritage.org.il

holysparks.com
innernet.org.il
israelnationalnews.com
israeltoday.co.il
jafi.org,il
jewfaq.org
jewishdatabank.org
jewishgates.com
jewishmediaresources.com
jewishpress.com
jewishvirtuallibrary.org
jpi.org
kehillastorah.org
kesser.org
maven.co.il
mlife.org
njop.org
ou.org
prayer4u.org
religionfacts.com
rickross.com
schuellerhouse.com
shemayisrael.co.il
simpletoremember.com
theshmuz.com
torah.org
ujc.org
worldpress.org
yeshiva.org.il

ABOUT THE AUTHOR

Margery Isis Schwartz is President of ASPEN RESEARCH, inc., a marketing research company located in Coral Gables, FL. (aspen-research.com). She has a Master of Science degree in Research, Testing, and Measurement.

Ms. Schwartz lives in Miami with her husband and cat, Cleo. She hopes that this book helps the world to remember that the behavior God is looking for from personkind is human consideration and acceptance.

"While I've written many client presentations over the years, I am a first-time author of a non-fiction book. However, my personal experience with being the mother of a ba'al teshuva, extensive background in conducting secondary and Internet research, and an endorsement by Aish HaTorah of the accuracy of the Jewish information should give me credibility."